POLICE, LAWYERS & JUDGES

Bullies with Power
A TRUE STORY

By
KIM R. DAVIS

© 2012 Kim R. Davis. All Rights Reserved

No part of this book may be reproduced or transmitted in any form or by any means, graphic, electronic, or mechanical, including photocopying recording, taping, or by any information storage retrieval system, without the written permission of the author.

To request Author Kim R. Davis for book signings, speaking engagements, or any other special events, please contact:

Kim R. Davis

Library of Congress Control Number: 2013912546
ISBN: 978-0-9860463-0-8

A WORD OF WISDOM

To God be the glory. Please, if you have not committed a crime, do not sign any paperwork at the police station, no matter how much pressure they put on you. Never take a guilty plea if you're innocent. Fight the good fight with the Father, Son, and Holy Ghost. Have good character and be the best friend, co-worker you can be. You never know who's going to be your character witness. It might be your boss. Get to work on time, do your job, and always have a bank account. A good lawyer will cost you $5,000. Don't worry about buying designer clothes when you're in jail. Nobody cares about the labels on your clothes. Teach your daughters how to be ladies and your sons how to be gentlemen. Teach respect. Please have them listen to "To Be Young Gifted and Black" by the late Donnie Hathaway and "We're a Winner" by the late Curtis Mayfield. Keep negative people away from you and your children. Jesus came so we can have life and have it more abundantly. If at all possible, get them involved in some kind of activity, like the arts, music, or sports. They need that discipline. My favorite Bible verse: "In all thy ways acknowledge him and he shall direct thy path." Never forget to hold on to God's unchanging hand. Peace and love with God. All things are possible!!!

Love and Peace,
Sister Kim Rose Davis

Special Thanks to:

The Father, the Son, and the Holy Ghost
Zack Davis, for teaching that the power lies inside of me
Ruby Davis Crawford, for being a Christian, praying mother
The late Pastor Lindell L. Brady
The late Dr. Martin Luther King Sr.
The late Roy I. Greer
Pastor Marvin A. Jennings
Pastor Emeritus Roosevelt Austin of Saginaw, Michigan
Pastor Tellis Chapman of Detroit, Michigan
Bishop Roger L. Jones Sr.
Elder Dana Chaney
Elder Theodore Files
Elder Dennis Walker
Reverend Bernice Haynes
Reverend Cary Brassfield
Reverend Kenneth R. Gillard
Pastor Lewis Randolph
Pastor Orlando Goodman
Bishop T. D. Jakes (for preaching "It Ain't Over")
Ferrald Waller
Frankie Ganway
Tonnie Johns
Kathy Battle
Minnie Buford
Carman Hill
Edward Green
Pierre Burnett
Robert Richards III
Michael Mavis
Melissa Blaque
Lee Black
Lamar Black
Joyce Black
Dorothy Black

Rosemary Turner
Juna Woodson
Sheila Chandler
Marilyn Wilson Smith
Carlos Boaz
Debbie Winston Roberts
Carnell Smith
Tex
Art
Antoinette Weathers
Dr. & Mrs. Billy Lewis aka godparents
Leroy Turner
L. C. Taylor

Yolanda Lamar Wilder, founder & president of Women Entrepreneurs of America

Quinton Bailey, thank you for being kind & just toward me during the most difficult time of my life

To all the writers, musicians, and singers whose music got me through and kept me uplifted

Police, Lawyers & Judges Bullies with Power

SPRING 2006. I JUST FINISHED WATCHING THE *OPRAH WINFREY SHOW*. I was too lazy to find the remote to change the channel, so I watched WMEN Channel Five News instead, which is the Saginaw and Bay City area news. I was shocked at what I saw—an African-American Buena Vista police officer in full uniform with his back turned to the camera. He was handcuffed as I listened to the charges, and he was being charged with rape. I thought back to a show I watched called *City Confidential,* narrated by the late Paul Winfield. There was an episode where a California highway patrol officer would stop women that were alone at night and have them follow him to a dark, secluded area off the freeway. He eventually killed a young lady. He was caught when he made a police video telling women how to be safe when they were alone at night and were getting pulled over. Women called into the news media and complained that he was the one that was pulling them over and leading them off the freeway. Then my mind started to wonder about how safe I was at night, since I work from midnight to 8:00 A.M., and I ride to work alone. I drive to Saginaw, Michigan, which is about a 25-mile drive.

After watching the news, I began to ready myself for my evening run at Flint Hamady High School. During my run, my mind started to wander again and question how safe I was. As I continued jogging,

I remembered an incident with my father when we were over at Flint Northern High School around the mid-eighties, watching a track meet. There were two young men there with pit bulls, and they kept dropping the leashes and walked away. I became afraid and told my father that I was leaving. He asked me why.

I told him that I was really afraid of the dogs!!! He told me I wasn't going anywhere, that he was my father and that he would protect me and would not let any harm or danger come to me, and that's when I truly realized that's what my Heavenly Father is to me. I started to praise GOD!!! A song by the late Rev. Charles Nicks ran through my mind, **"I CAN DEPEND ON GOD!!"** "Through the storm, through the rain, through sickness and pain, I can depend, I can depend, I can depend, I can truly depend on GOD!!!" As I finished singing one of my favorite songs, I thought of my two grandmothers, the late Mrs. Lenora Black and Mrs. Nellie E. Parker. Their favorite song was by the late great Mahalia Jackson, "Precious Lord."

Their favorite Bible verses were Psalm 23: "The **LORD** is my shepherd; I shall not want. **2** He maketh me to lie down in green pastures: he leadeth me beside the still waters. **3** He restoreth my soul: he leadeth me in the paths of righteousness for his name's sake. **4** Yea, though I walk through the valley of the shadow of death, I will fear no evil: for thou art with me; thy rod and thy staff they comfort me. **5** Thou preparest a table before me in the presence of mine enemies; thou anointest my head with oil; my cup runneth over. **6** Surely goodness and mercy shall follow me all the days of my life; and I will dwell in the house of the **LORD** for ever."

After I finished praising, singing, and worshiping, I realized how relaxing praying and running is. I would encourage each and every one of you to praise **GOD** when you feel lost, walk, or run. It will renew your mind and give you strength, because without **GOD**, you cannot make it.

September 15, 2006. As I awakened, my heart was very heavy. Today was the funeral of my uncle, the late Dr. Stanley A. Turner, MD. He was such a loving husband and father. He had such a close bond with his daughter, LT. My heart was extremely heavy for her in losing such a great man of integrity. As I began to visualize all of the accomplishments that my uncle Stan had achieved—he was the first African-American baseball player for Michigan State University, he was the first African-American to play at Duke University, he was the leading hitter, batting 333 in nine games during the Southern Tour—he never would discuss the racism that he endured and how he wasn't able to stay in hotels with his teammates. He had to stay with black families.

In 1954, he signed a pro contract with the Cleveland Indians for $4,000 a year. He returned to Michigan State University to fulfill his dream of becoming a medical doctor. He graduated from the college of human medicine and specialized in family medicine. Dr. Turner held a solo private practice in Hartford, Connecticut, until his retirement.

After thinking about Uncle Stan, I decided that I should not be sad about his death; instead, I was going to celebrate his life. After visualizing all the accomplishments he made, I started to sing **"WHAT A MAN, WHAT A MIGHTY GOOD MAN,"** by Salt-N-Pepa featuring En Vogue.

Instead of choosing a black pantsuit, I chose to wear orange, and this color represents power. Orange is one of the healing colors. It is said it also stimulates enthusiasm and creativity, and means vitality with endurance. Uncle Stan was very creative, and there would have not been any other color to represent his life but orange, baby!!!

Once I was in my vehicle, I reached into my CD case for one of my old jazz CDs. Uncle Stan was an avid jazz listener. I selected this song to represent his life, titled, "Song for My Father" by Horace Silver.

> If there was ever a man
> Who was generous, gracious and good
> That was my dad
> The man
> A human being so true
> He could live like a king,
> 'Cause he knew the real pleasure in life
> To be devoted to
> And always stand by me
> So I'd be unafraid and free

If there was ever a man who was generous, gracious and good
That was my dad
The man
A human being so true
He could live like a king
'Cause he knew
The real pleasure in life
To be devoted to
And always stand by me
So I'd be not afraid and free
If there was ever a man
Who was generous, gracious and good
That was my dad
The man,
The man.

I started to think of all the great men in my life that molded me to be a respectable black female, to treat everybody with love and kindness, knowing that what you give out you would get back in return: my uncles Renzealous Woodson, Oscar, Eddie, and Mark Woodson, which were my grandmother's brothers. My father also taught me how to eat healthy and never to be a victim, to fight back, and how to use what you have in your hand to your best advantage. How to use your keys and feet as weapons and always to scan the parking lot before getting out of your vehicle. I learned never park by a van and always watch and make sure, especially at night, to see if anyone is following you for an extended amount of time, and to go to a lighted public place. I started to think of the late Pastor Emeritus Lindell L. Brady, of the GEBC, which I joined at the tender age of 11—one of the best decisions of my life.

Pastor Emeritus Brady taught me how to love the Lord with all my heart, how to study the Word of **GOD**, to know who you are and that you belong to the Father, Son, and Holy Ghost. He also taught me to always keep **GOD** in my heart at all times, to always have a job so that I can have money in my pocket for a rainy day, to be the best person that I can be for **GOD** and my community. He taught me to always take a stand for righteousness, because if you don't, you will fall for anything. He was an avid chess player and taught the youth fellowship fundamentals of chess so that we could make wise decisions in our everyday life. Chess gives you a critical thinking ability. He was also a fisherman and hunter and taught me how to ride a horse. He and the late Deacon Robert Richardson II would take the youth fellowship department to Bay City, Michigan, to ride horses. I was afraid my first time there, but my pastor told me I was a child of God and to never fear anything. With that, I got on the black-and-white horse and rode as if I had been riding my whole life. When I rode next to my pastor, he asked me if I was okay. I replied yes, and with that, my pastor took off riding that horse as if he was the black John Wayne starring in a Western. I tapped my horse on his behind and took off after my pastor. When I arrived at the stable, my pastor was pleasantly surprised that I finished my ride not too far behind him.

The one thing I admired about the late Pastor Brady was that he forced me to use my voice. I was extremely shy, and my two sisters always spoke for me. I would just stand back and not speak because my aunts and uncles would laugh at me. I could not pronounce *refrigerator* as a child. My aunts and uncles would point at the refrigerator and ask me what it was, and I would mess up that word, and then they would laugh. I had one aunt call me "Big Nose Kim Rose." She grabbed a measuring tape, informing me I had the biggest nose in the house. Can you imagine what that did to my self-esteem? But, I had a pastor that was full of knowledge and wisdom, who saw the pain of my childhood on my face. I felt so ugly that I wanted to be invisible. I always stood behind my two sisters, and my oldest sister would speak for me.

Once, we were in an Usher board meeting, and I wanted to ask a question, so I whispered to my older sister, the late Krystal Davis Wright. My pastor saw me whisper to my sister, and when my sister stood up, he sat her down and said, "Kim can speak. I would love to hear Kim's voice today. Kim has a voice that was given to her by **GOD**. Speak, Sister Kim." I stood up and spoke in church for the first time. At the age of 11, he would force me to look him in his eyes when I shook his hand after Sunday services because my head was always hung down. He would ask me questions like, "Sister Kim, what color are my shoes?" I would tell him the color of his shoes, and then he would tell me to look him in his eyes while speaking to him. When you are a child of **GOD**, you are somebody important. It doesn't matter if your nose is big or you can't enunciate *refrigerator* correctly. You are **SOMEBODY TO GOD AND NEVER FORGET IT!!!!!**

On September 1977, the late Pastor Lindell L. Brady gave the congregation a gift that I will never forget. I had the opportunity to meet the late Dr. Martin Luther King Sr. I shook hands with history, and my heart was elated all day long.

On September 28, 2006, the night of my arrest, it was a beautiful fall night. The moon was glowing as if it were sunlight. As I started my commute to my third-shift job, I did the usual. I stopped at the store to pick up the newspaper. As I looked into the store, I saw two males standing there. The clerk was a female. As she looked out the window toward my vehicle, I thought something was wrong so I grabbed my dog spray and placed it in my right front jacket pocket, and I counted to 10 as I walked into the store. I prayed to the Lord that if something was wrong, she and I would get out of this situation alive.

Once I got inside the store, the two males walked out. I asked her if she was okay, and she said yes. She stated they were asking her out. I replied, "Okay, I came in here to help." She said thanks, then I returned to my vehicle and put in my *Chaka Khan Greatest Hits* CD. I love listening to Chaka Khan.

Once I got on the Birch Run Exit, I looked to the left to see if the Michigan state police cruiser was in his regular spot. He was, so I blew the horn at him, and he blew back. As I traveled north on Interstate 75, I noticed two more Michigan state police officers traveling the same way as I. I thought it must be ticket time so I set my cruise at 66 mph. The speed limit was 70 mph. I was making sure that they did not have a reason to pull me over. Once I got to my exit, 149 B Holland Drive, the song "I'm Every Woman" was playing in the background. I was singing along with Chaka Khan.

Upon exiting off the highway, I noticed something was out of order. The previous four nights there were two police vehicles parked at a restaurant called the Texan. Only one was parked in the hotel parking lot to my right, which was on the corner of Holland and Outer Drive. His vehicle was under the third light facing north. I looked over at him and realized he was African-American. I was wondering why he was sitting in a hotel parking lot.

As I made a right onto Outer Drive traveling north to my job, as soon as my headlights approached the entrance to the hotel parking lot, the lights on the police cruiser came on. I glanced over at the officer and wondered what the emergency was. As I turned onto Outer Drive, I set my cruise control at 30 mph. The speed limit was 35 mph.

I traveled north on Outer Drive, and then I glanced up and saw the police cruiser with all the lights flashing, headed my way. He was driving extremely fast, as if he had a serious emergency to get to. I pulled over to the right side of the road to give him the right-of-way. I noticed he never passed me. Instead, he stopped behind me. I became frightened. My heart was beating rapidly, and my hands were sweating profusely. I really didn't know what to do. I started thinking he was going to take me back to the hotel and rape me. He must be the rapist that I saw on TV. Then I remembered there's a store north of here on the left-hand side on Janes and Outer Dr. I proceeded up the street doing 25 mph so he would know I was not running from him, that I was just driving to a lighted area and hoped that people were around, in case he might be the rapist. As we were traveling on Outer Drive, coming from the left was another cruiser, so now there were two police cruisers traveling behind me at a slow rate of speed. After I reached my destination on Janes and Outer, I came to a complete stop underneath a streetlight.

I looked to my left at the store named Stop and Shop, and to my dismay, nobody was in the parking lot. At that moment, I heard a voice instructing me to **GET OUT OF THE CAR!!!** I got out of my car with my hands up in the air just like I saw people do on the TV cop shows. The African-American looked to be between the ages of 27–33. He stood between 5 foot 9 and 5 foot 11 and weighed about 240 pounds. His skin was dark. The Caucasian looked to be between 40–45. He was between 6 foot 2 and 6 foot 4 and weighed about 265 pounds.

As they approached me, the African-American officer hollered at me saying, "Are you high or looking for drugs?"

I replied, "No, what do you want?"

He repeated again, "Are you high or looking for drugs?"

Again, I replied, "No, I told you the first time, and no, for the second time, now what do you want?"

He repeated it again for the third time, "Are you high or looking for drugs?"

I refused to answer; instead, I asked him, "What is your probable cause?"

He didn't reply at all. The Caucasian officer asked me why I didn't stop. I explained to him, I did stop, but I was afraid. Newscasters on TV tell women that are driving alone at night to be safe and secure at your stop, and that's all I had done. The Caucasian police officer looked directly at me and hollered, "You might have that right in other places, but when you are in Buena Vista, you ain't got no rights. I don't care if it's dark and you don't understand what we want. You pull over!!!!" As he pointed his finger in my face, he said, "You pull over immediately and **STOP!!!**"

I went from frightened to furious. After listening to Chaka Khan's "I'm Every Woman," I was ready to put him in his place, so I looked up at him, and I raised my voice to the same level of loudness as his, and said, "**YOU ARE A LIAR!!!** I know my rights, and I have the right to drive up and down Outer Dr. as many times as I want as long as I am doing the speed limit, and you don't have the right to bother me. **NOW WHAT DO YOU IDIOTS WANT???**"

There was silence as he stood staring at me with hatred in his eyes. I was stared back at him holding my ground. He looked at me as though he wanted to hit me. I thought I was going to have to fight this man. I tried to remember everything my father taught me about martial arts and my late uncle Lewis Black and Charlie Copeland, who were both boxers. I decided to try to drop low on this big boy and tackle him, but at that moment he asked for my identification so I gave him my workplace ID. He wrote my birth date on his wrist and went back to the first cruiser to run my information.

The African-American officer told me to spread my legs with my hands on top of the roof of the vehicle. I replied, "**NO!**"

He asked, "What did you say to me?"

Police, Lawyers & Judges

I answered, "I am not doing it. You haven't told me what criminal act I've committed. What's your probable cause?" I asked.

He answered, "Huh?"

I replied, "You heard me, you can't stop me because you feel like it, and you have to have a probable cause."

He then replied, "The light over your license plate is out."

I replied, **"YOU ARE A LIAR!!!** You couldn't see the back of my car from where you were parked, plus, I passed three state police officers before you, so I know you are **LYING!!!"**

I started walking to the back of my car when he asked, "Where you are going?"

I said, "To prove to you that you are a **LIAR!!!"**

Once I reached the back of my vehicle the light was lit over my license plate. I looked at him and said, "You **LYING JACKASS!!!"** I turned toward the cruiser where the Caucasian officer was seated in his car behind my vehicle, and I said, "Give me my ID. You are causing me to be late for work, and you are playing games. It's costing me **MONEY!** Now I am going to have to explain to my supervisor why I am late."

The Caucasian officer told the African-American officer to cuff me. I turned around and put my hands behind my back and told him to cuff me. "I'm still going to work. I will just be late because I am clean. You'll find that out after you run my information."

He placed me in the backseat, and then he sat in the front seat. About 3–5 minutes passed, then I heard a voice come over the radio. The speaker spoke in a very disappointed tone. "That's her car. Yes, it's insured; no warrants, no priors."

The African-American officer turned around and looked at me and told me he knows a crackhead when he sees one. "I'm going to search your car for drugs."

As I tried to tell him no, he jumped out of the car and slammed the door and ran toward my vehicle. Next, I heard the Caucasian officer saying, **"GET HER ASS!! GET HER ASS!!! GET SOMETHING ON HER ASS!!!"**

The African-American officer shook his head and asked, "There's nothing in her vehicle?"

The Caucasian officer was upset, so he ran to the trunk of my car and popped it open. They went through my bowling bag and my pool stick. They touched my alkaline water which is in clear jugs. The Caucasian officer became elated and said, **"WE GOT HER ASS! SHE'S HAULING MOONSHINE!!!"** They opened up the jugs, smelled them, and tasted them. They were disappointed again as they walked back toward the cruiser where I was seated in the back. The window was rolled down.

Then I asked the big Caucasian officer, **"WHO HAS WHOSE ASS NOW? I HAVE YOUR ASS!!!** That was nothing but water, you silly **ASSHOLE.** Can I go to work **NOW???"**

He looked in the cruiser at me and said, **"NO, YO MOMMA!!!"**

I started to laugh at that moment. Then the back passenger-side door opened, and a Hispanic female officer told me how to get out of the car. Once I was out of the vehicle, she closed the door. I was just standing there as she pushed me on my right shoulder with her left hand. I told her not to push me, just tell me what to do. I had never been in this position before so I just started walking. She wouldn't tell me what to do, and this time she pushed me in the middle of my back, causing me to stumble. I turned around and told her to **STOP IT!!**

She said to me, "Are you a street woman? You go for tough in the streets?"

"No," I replied. "I am not a street woman. I am a workingwoman as you are. I pay taxes just as you do."

At that moment, another cruiser approached. A tall Caucasian officer stepped out. He was to the left of me and stood maybe 6 foot 4. He had a slender build and was leaning on the driver-side door. He asked the other Caucasian officer, "What's the problem?"

The other officer replied, "She thinks she has the right to stop wherever she wants to."

At that moment I stopped walking to see if he was going to say, "If that's all this is about, then let her go."

At that moment, I felt a hand at the base of my neck and right above my buttocks, then into the police cruiser I went flying. In the midst of my flight, I turned myself to the right to keep my face from slamming into the side of the cruiser. I allowed my right shoulder to receive the force of the impact. Once I got off the cruiser, I looked to my left to see if the new officer on the scene would take me away from these Three Stooges. Instead, he got in his vehicle and turned south on Outer Drive as though he was running away from the scene of the crime. I felt hands on my body as the female officer was searching me. She reached in my right front jacket pocket and found some dog spray and handed it to the Caucasian officer. Then she turned me around so that I was facing her. I gave her the meanest look and thought to myself, *If this was on equal ground, I would destroy her!!!* I looked her over real good, giving her a look to kill!!! She was about 5 foot 6 and weighed 160 pounds. She was backing up and told me to follow her. We didn't take our eyes off each other. I looked her in eyes to let her know that I had no fear in me and that she's a coward to slam someone while in handcuffs. She placed me in the back of the cruiser.

The Caucasian officer told the African-American officer to write me up for carrying a concealed weapon, and his reply was "Huh?"

The Caucasian officer said, "You heard me!!!"

The African-American officer looked at him again and repeated, "Huh??"

The Caucasian officer placed his left arm on the driver-side door and had his right arm waving toward the street. He asked the African-American officer, "Do you see any dogs running around here?"

The African-American officer replied, "No!!"

The Caucasian officer replied, "There ain't no dogs. That makes it a concealed weapon." He saw me looking at his mouth and told the African-American officer, "Get out of the car. I want to talk to you where she can't hear." They went to the front of the vehicle and the African-American officer, with his back facing east, his hands clasped behind the back of his head, was nodding up and down as though he was saying, **"YES, SIR!!!"**

The Caucasian officer was yelling, his right hand was balled into a fist, his left hand was opened, and he was hitting his left palm continually. This went on for 5 minutes. Once he stopped all of his yelling, he turned and faced me. He was staring at me with a very evil expression on his face.

At that moment, the front-passenger door opened, and the African-American ducked his head in with a big grin on his face. "Guess where you are going," he said. I didn't reply. His smile disappeared and he hollered, **"YOU ARE GOING TO JAIL!!!"**

I looked at the front of the vehicle at the big Caucasian officer. He was looking at me waiting for a reaction. I thought to myself, *They want to see me cry and beg for mercy. Well, they have the wrong black woman.* "Vengeance is mine, thus says the Lord." Just like in Esther chapter 7, verses 9–10, "And Harbonah, one of the chamberlains, said before the king, Behold also, the gallows fifty cubits high, which Haman had made for Mordecai, who had spoken good for the king, standeth in the house of Haman. Then the king said, Hang him thereon. So they hanged Haman on the gallows that he had prepared for Mordecai. Then was the king's wrath pacified."

HAMAN SET A trap for Mordecai, but he ended up being hung in the trap that he had set for Mordecai, so these Three Stooges better beware. When **GOD** gets tired of their silliness, they will reap what they sow.

As we were seated in the cruiser waiting for the tow truck driver, I asked this silly immature African-American male officer to please get my boss's number out of my vehicle. I told him it's in the front of my lunch container on a yellow sheet of paper. He told me **NO**. I again said, "Please, since you are taking me to jail I need to call my boss and let him know what my situation is."

He replied, "When you get your one phone call from the jail call him from there."

"Yes, I will call him from jail as you stated, but I don't know his number!!! Can you please get the yellow paper??"

He replied, "I don't care about you or your job."

At that moment the tow truck appeared. A Caucasian man stepped out of the truck. He was between 5 foot 7 and 5 foot 9 and wore glasses. He had on blue or black clothing and some type of white lettering on his jacket. The African-American officer jumped out of the cruiser laughing, saying, "Guess what I got in the backseat? Your girlfriend."

The Caucasian man and African-American officer approached the back door of the vehicle where I was seated. The African-American officer opened the door, pointed at me, and said, **"YOUR GIRLFRIEND!!"**

The Caucasian male looked in the cruiser. I saw his name tag on his jacket. It read Nate, and he said, "I don't want her. You can have her." Then they slammed the door closed as they both began to laugh.

After the laughter he hooked up my vehicle and towed my car away. I was looking at the light over the license plate. It was lit. I felt as if I were in the *Twilight Zone*, waiting for Rod Sterling to end this episode so I could go to work. Finally, this ignorant African-American officer got in the cruiser. I asked him, "Did you think that was funny what you just did? How dare you demean my character."

He answered, "It's funny. I'm laughing, ain't I?"

"Do you think a white man would demean a white woman to a black man as you did to me?"

He replied, **"SHUT UP!!"** Then he turned the cruiser around facing south and picked up his two-way radio and asked someone, "What should I charge her with?"

A voice responded with code numbers 0203, 0207, 0205, 0208, or something to that effect. I thought to myself, *This guy is an idiot. He doesn't know what he's taking me to jail for.* He made a right-hand turn onto Janes heading west and looked in the mirror and said, "Hey, you." I didn't reply. He said it again, "Hey, you."

I answered, "What do you want?"

"Why did you talk back to him? He doesn't like people to talk back to him."

I replied, "Let me explain something to you. I was on my way to work, not bothering you or him. I will speak back to him anyway I feel. I committed no crime. That's why I talked back to him. This is 2006 not 1896. **I HAVE RIGHTS!!!** Plus, this is nothing but driving while black."

He continued to drive, maybe around 8–10 minutes, then he made a right-hand turn, but I could not see the name of the street. Another 3–5 minutes of traveling north. Finally, I did notice to my left the Saginaw Children's Zoo. The cross street was Washington Avenue. As we continued north, I noticed beautiful lights to the right of me. I figured out this must be Ojibwa Island. My co-workers speak about. It is really pretty at night.

Just as I was enjoying my view of the island he turned and looked at me saying, "I am going to play you some soul music because I am going to put you away for a long time!" He turned on the radio. The song playing was Kindred the Family Soul, "Where Would I Be." He turned the radio off when he realized I was enjoying the music.

For the first time I wanted to turn into Bruce Lee and kick him in the back of head and maybe kick some sense into it!! So I asked him, "Where do you live at?"

He replied, "Are you out of your **RABBIT MIND?** I am not going to tell you where I live!"

So I told him, "I want to ring your doorbell and let you know I am out of jail and that you have no power over me. All power belongs to GOD and not you. When he's ready to release me, I will be set free."

He replied, **"SHUT UP!!"**

I noticed a big clock to my left. It was the courthouse. Once we pulled in the jail drop-off area he opened the door so I could get out. I started to walk toward the door, but he grabbed my left arm above the elbow, turned me to face him, and made a big ugly face. He told me that I have a smart mouth and the next time he sees me, he's going to use a Taser on me. I just stared at him and that seemed to annoy him, so he squeezed my arm tighter and his face got uglier, and hollered at me, **"DO YOU HEAR ME? I WILL ELECTROCUTE YOU!!!"**

I looked up and noticed cameras. I thought to myself, *He's trying to get a witness on me talking back to,* so I smiled at him. He tossed me back toward the cruiser with enough force to stun me but not hurt me. Then he grabbed me by my left arm and pulled me inside the jail. Once inside, he started screaming, **"TELL THOSE PEOPLE WHAT YOU HAVE BEEN SMOKING AND DRINKING!!"** He hollered it again.

I started scanning the room. My father always said a good soldier observes each and every small detail when they enter into enemy territory. I noticed a female Caucasian jail guard, 5 foot 9, slender, with brown hair pulled in a ponytail, standing to my right. I saw two glass jail cells to my right, three to four black males occupying the first cell. They were standing up. The second jail cell was occupied by two white females lying on the floor. To my left was a counter and seated behind the counter were three male jail guards. One was a male African-American, quite dark, wearing gold-rimmed glasses. He was small, maybe 5 foot 7 and probably weighed between 140–155 pounds. He sat near the window.

I noticed five sheets of white paper on the counter. The African-American police officer threw me against the counter where the five sheets of white paper rested. He then placed his forearm in the middle of my back as he started screaming at me to sign the five sheets of paper. Spit flew out of his mouth, so I turned my face to the left. Next thing I know, he came over to my left and yelled, **"SIGN THESE PAPERS!!!"**

I started pleading with my eyes at the gentleman seated near the window to get him off of me. A few more times of this outrageous behavior from the African-American Buena Vista police officer, then I finally felt a hand on my right arm. It was a young lady that was standing against the wall. She told me to come with her and led me to a room. Once inside the room, she said that I have two felonies on me.

I replied, "Okay."

Next, she handed me an orange uniform.

I asked, "What is this for?"

Her response was, "For you to put on. You have felonies on you, and you can't go anywhere."

I replied, "Okay," then I thought to myself, *I don't know what felonies are, but I will just play it cool.*

Next, she told me to bend over and spread my buttocks cheeks. I asked if she was serious. She said drugs could be stashed there. I felt violated, but I bent over and spread them like she told me. She said I can keep my bra on if it doesn't have any underwire that could be used for a weapon. She took my socks from me, and I slipped my feet into a pair of orange flip-flops.

Finally, she said, "Let's go."

I said, "Wait, do you have a mirror?"

She asked, "What do you need a mirror for?"

I told her the African-American officer was still out there and he wanted to see tears and snot running down my face, but I was only going to show him black beauty. She told me she didn't have a mirror, so I asked her if my lipstick was still on, and she said yes, so I licked my lips to give them a fresh shine, and I positioned myself to walk out the door as if I were on the runway and I was the most fierce model of them all.

She opened the door. I stepped out. There he was, leaned up against the wall facing the door that I had to walk out of, so I gave him the walk of the most beautiful, boisterous strong black woman on this planet. Naomi Campbell, a famous model, didn't have anything on me. I worked my hips to the east and to the west. I was following her and staring at him. He had the most bewildered look on his face. He could not believe he couldn't break me. I wanted to make sure he told the other Two Stooges that they couldn't break me, either.

As I was led into the holding cell, I stood at the door watching him as he continued to stare for about 2 minutes. He turned to leave, but he turned back again and glanced once more time at me, and I blew him a kiss!!! Finally, he turned away and left. I began to look for somewhere to sit, but nothing was there except a concrete floor.

I spoke to my two cell mates. One looked to be between 4 foot 11 and 5 foot 1 with red curly hair, probably 115 pounds, and around the age of 40. The other cell mate was 5 foot 2, 200 pounds, and around the age of 19–21. I asked them, "Where's the benches or chairs?"

Their reply was, "This is what we walked into, nothing but a concrete floor!!"

"Isn't this illegal?" I asked.

The redhead replied, "It should be. I been in jail before, but I have never seen something like this."

I stood for as long as I could, and then I had to use the bathroom so I asked my cell mates, "How do you get a guard to take you to the restroom?"

She pointed and said, "The toilet is behind the wall."

I turned and look toward the wall. It was no taller than 3 foot 5 inches. I asked, "Can't the men behind the desk see you?"

"They can if they come from the north of the building. If no one does, then they cannot see you."

I told them I was going to hold it as long as I could, because there was no privacy. We talked and both of them told me why they were here. When they asked me why I was here, I told them I didn't know. They told me I had to know because I had on orange clothing.

"They just told me I was going to jail and never told me why."

The redhead asked me a question. "Did they read you your rights?"

I replied, **"NO!"**

"It's hard to believe that no one read you your rights and you don't know why you are here."

I replied, "**YES**, that's the truth. The African-American officer just stated, 'You are going to **JAIL!!!**'"

At that moment, I heard my name being called by a young, dark-haired Caucasian male. He was asking me when the last time was that I had been in jail.

I answered him, "Never."

He told me I was a liar, that the African-American officer told him I was a repeated offender.

My reply was, "Look it up and tell me so we all will know about it." He gave me a look of disgust.

I took my seat on the concrete floor. Soon, entering our cell was a Hispanic female wearing blue jeans, a white tank top, and no shoes. Her dark hair was a little past her shoulders. She looked to be around 25–32. She stood at 5 foot 5 and weighed 150 pounds. I could smell alcohol on her breath. She took a seat next to me and told me she's mad at all Caucasian females, so I asked her why. Her reply was she was at the bar singing karaoke and two Caucasian girls were flirting with her boyfriend, so she took a pitcher of beer and threw it at the girls, and then they got into a fight.

I asked, "What happened to your shoes?"

She replied, "I threw them too!!"

I started laughing and asked her, "Why didn't you leave the bar? Why did you wait for the police?"

She replied, "I was kicking their tails, and it felt good and I couldn't stop."

The next thing she remembered was the police pulling her off of them. At that moment, they came for my two other cell mates. She asked me what happened to me. So I told her, then she asked me if I wanted her to help fight them, but I told her no. She said, "But I can

FIGHT!!" She tried to explain to me what store she worked at so I could pick her up, and then we can fight the police officers together.

I told her, "No, I'm going to fight through the legal system."

She replied, "You're really not from here, are you?"

I said, "No!! I wasn't playing when I said I live in Genesee County."

She replied, "Let me tell you something, there is no justice in Saginaw."

I answered, "Saginaw can't be any different than any other city."

She said, "Look at this concrete floor you are sitting on. It's illegal!!! And wait until they lock you up in the bathroom downstairs."

I didn't believe her so I didn't say anything else. After that, we just turned the conversation to everyday talk. After a couple of hours of being there, they took her to the front desk and told her she could make her telephone call and leave. She came back to the cell and asked me, "Have you made your telephone call?"

I told her no. At that moment, a short, stocky man with sandy-brown hair came for me. He took me to the front desk where the dark-haired young man from earlier was seated. He had some papers for me to sign. I glanced down at them. I asked him for my reading glasses. He said, "What did you say???"

I said, "Young man, I need my reading glasses."

He told the sandy-brown haired young man to take me back to my cell. "I am not dealing with your attitude."

I said, "Young man, I am not giving you attitude. I am 50 years old. I need my reading glasses. You locked them up and put them in an envelope. All I am simply asking is for my glasses. That is one of my rights, isn't it? I have the right to read before I sign the papers. This is not an attitude; it's a right."

He looked up at the stocky guy and told him to get me away from him. "I am not dealing with her!!!!"

The young man looked at me and him. I said to him, "Just get my glasses and it will be the end of this drama."

He screamed, **"GET HER AWAY FROM ME NOW!!!!"**

I looked at him with disbelief, but it came to me that he was the young man the African-American officer was standing near and talking to. The officer must have told him something about me, and he believed it. I went back to my cell. My cell mate asked if I was okay; if not, she would get him on her way out. I started laughing. I told her I will be okay.

Half an hour later, she's able to leave. We hugged and said it was nice meeting each other. She told me again where she worked, and if I needed anything, to come get her before she leaves. The Hispanic female went to the desk and told the dark-headed young man that I am a nice lady and was on my way to work and that I worked at Saginaw Metal Cast Operations and was 5 minutes away from my job when the Buena Vista police kidnapped me. She said, "Now you treat her nice."

He didn't reply; he just stared at her. She gave me a thumbs-up and left. Now I was alone for the first time. I took that time to apologize to the Lord for using the word *asshole*. I know that wasn't representing the Lord to the best of my ability. I will never let emotions come over me the way I did again.

After a few hours of sitting on the floor staring at the water fountain, I wanted a drink so bad I just could taste water. It seemed like eternity before a tall, bald-headed male entered my cell wearing glasses. He had blue eyes. He handed me a brown paper bag. I asked him, "What is it?"

He said, "It's five o'clock; it's your breakfast."

So I looked in the bag. It contained two sandwiches, one orange, and some type of frozen drink, around four ounces. I looked up at him. "May I please get a drink from the water fountain?" I asked.

He looked at me strangely and said, "What did you say?"

I looked up at him and repeated, **"MAY I PLEASE GET A DRINK OF WATER?"**

He said, "Sure," and he let me drink until my thirst was eliminated. When I walked back into my cell I thanked him. He asked me again, "What did you just say to me??"

I replied, "Thank you."

He said, "You are welcome."

I also thanked him for being kind to me. He turned around and walked out, shaking his head. As I was eating my dry bologna sandwich, my cell door opened again. It was the same man who allowed me to have a drink of water. He said, "Come with me."

I followed him. He took me to an orange couch and told me to have a seat. He asked me if there's anything on TV that I would like to look at. I told him what's on is fine with me, then I asked him if there was a bathroom I can use.

He said sure and pointed me to the bathroom which had a door on it. I was so elated. Later, I chilled out, sitting with my legs up, relaxing. Soon, here comes the dark-headed mean young man asking, "Why is she out??"

The bald-headed man replied, "She's harmless. **LEAVE HER ALONE!!** If you have a problem with it, send someone to clean the cell." He walked to his seat and didn't say another word.

Finally, the African-American male seated near the window called me to him. He fingerprinted me and asked me in a voice just above a whisper, "What happened out there?" So I shared with him my story. He said, "I thought so. An officer never comes in and hangs around like he did and talk about you in the manner that he did. That's very unusual. Get yourself a good lawyer. I been watching you, and I don't see any of the traits he described. You are not drunk or violent or high."

I told him, "Thank you, and I will be getting myself a lawyer."

He placed a wristband on me that read Inmate Number #140409.

The kind officer called me to him so he could take my picture. He was telling me jokes to make me laugh. As this was going on, the dark-headed mean young man was observing everything going on. I took my seat back on the couch. After maybe 15 minutes, the nurse called me. She asked me what drugs I'd been using. She was standing next to the dark-headed young man.

I answered her, "Ma'am, I don't use drugs or use alcoholic beverages."

She looked up at me. I asked her, "Can't you tell? Look at my skin and eyes."

She said, "I had to ask you that because the officer who dropped you off stated that." She said, "I am sorry if I offended you."

I said, "No problem, I'm okay."

As I turned to walk back to the couch, the dark-headed mean young man asked me if I still needed my glasses. I said, "Yes, if you want me to sign what you had before."

He got my reading glasses. I read over the documents that he handed me. They wanted to know my place of employment. Then he asked me if I had made my telephone call. I told him no, so he pointed to the telephone and asked if I wanted to call my job. I told him, "No, the officer wouldn't let me get my boss's number." I looked at the clock. It was 5:30 A.M. I tried to think of someone to call that was already awake. I thought of my best friend Tonnie J. She started work at 6:00 A.M., so I called her. When she answered, I told her, "This is not a joke. Please listen to me closely. I'm in jail."

She didn't believe me. "You're at work," she said.

"No, listen to me, I'm in the Saginaw County Jail."

"For what?" she asked.

I told her, "I don't know." So I turned to the dark-headed young man and asked, "What am I here for?"

"Don't you know?" he responded.

"NO, I don't."

He told me I have five charges on me. "What are they I asked?"

He said, "Number 1, **CCW**."

I asked, "What is a CCW?"

He started laughing. "You mean to tell me you don't know what it is?"

"No, I don't. What is it?"

He said I either had a gun or a knife. I said, "No, I had dog spray."

"Number 2. Fleeing and Eluding."

I asked, "What is that?"

He responded, laughing, "A car chase."

I said, "I drove to a lighted area doing 25 mph. How is that eluding?"

He said, "Are you telling me the truth?"

I said, "Yes!!"

He said, "If you don't know, why are you here?"

I answered, "I got smart with a Caucasian officer that illegally stopped me and told me I have no rights."

"Then there needs to be an investigation."

So I told Tonnie J., "I am here on bogus charges. Get some money and please get me out!!"

She replied, "Kim, I am from Detroit. I don't have a clue where the jail is in Saginaw. You are about 80 miles north of me. Do you have directions?"

I said, "No, I've never been here before. I don't know where it is. Look it up on the computer and come get me out of here. I will pay you back."

She said, "What I'm going to do is call your mother."

I said, "No, don't call her. My whole life growing up my mother said, 'If you ever go to jail don't call me.'"

"Kim, these are bogus charges. I'm going to call your mother."

"All right," I replied and gave her my mother's telephone number. "Make sure you tell her the charges are bogus. I have not done anything."

We ended the telephone call. I went back to the couch and sat there until 6:00 A.M. The young lady from earlier told me to follow her. I turned around and waved good-bye to the bald-headed gentleman and told him thanks for his kindness. He smiled at me and told me bye.

I followed the woman to an area where there was a big stack of orange mats on the left-hand side. She told me to reach down and get one. I asked, "Are they sanitized?"

She didn't reply to my question. She simply told me I have to get one. I reached and got one, then she led me to a door. When she opened the door I saw only darkness and felt cold air. She told me I have to go inside. I didn't want to. I was afraid. Then I heard a familiar voice. It was one of the two women that were upstairs with me.

I turned and looked at the jail guard asking, "Do I really have to go in there?"

She replied, "Yes, you do!!"

I dragged my mat and stepped inside. It felt like a freezer. She slammed the door. I heard the door lock. I stood there for a moment. For the first time I was truly afraid. I was cold. It was dark, and the only light was from the small window in the door with light coming from the bottom crack of the door.

There was another young lady there. She told me to place my mat on the floor and said I will be okay, so I lay there, and I was shivering. My feet were freezing. I wanted my socks back so badly. I tried to go to sleep, but I couldn't. My foot kept hitting something extremely cold. I didn't know what it was. I got up to investigate and found out it was a toilet. I realized I was locked up in a bathroom. This has *got* to be illegal. I was thinking to myself, after all, I'm in America. You wouldn't think this would be allowed, Then I started hoping that none of us have a bowel movement because the smell would linger.

Finally, it was 11:00 A.M. The door opened. Two female African-American jail guards passed out lunch. One was 5 foot 5 with a light complexion. Her hair was pulled back in a ponytail. She weighed around 210 pounds and wore light-colored glasses and looked to be in her mid-forties. The other one had a short, cute haircut. Her skin complexion looked like the color of caramel candy. She was attractive, but her demeanor was so harsh she became ugly to me. She might have been a size 8. Her height was around 5 foot 5, and her face frowned up she spoke. Her tone was harsh as she spoke to the other cell mates. *She's wicked,* I thought.

I asked her for a blanket. She started hollering, **"NO, YOU CAN'T HAVE A BLANKET!!!"**

I asked for my socks. Her response was, **"NO!!!"**

I asked her if she could tell me if I was going to be arraigned today. She told me, "Why don't you just shut up?"

Then I asked her how much longer would I have to be in this cold, dark, dreary room. She replied, "If you don't shut up we will hold you here 72 hours." So I decided to shut up. She recognized the young lady who was not my cell mate from earlier that night. She started hollering at her, asking her what she was doing back here.

The young lady replied, "I didn't catch a new case. I'm here because I dropped dirty."

She proceeded to berate the young lady, then she slammed the door shut. You could hear the key lock it. It was a horrible feeling. I turned to the young lady and asked the question, "What do you mean you 'dropped dirty'?"

She replied, "I'm on probation, and I smoked some weed."

I said, "OK, I just wondered."

I decided to stand up. I stood up for as long as I could. I tried to run in place. This dark, cold room was getting the best of me. I was trying to generate some heat, but after awhile, my legs were aching; in fact, my buttocks, back, and shoulders all were aching. I'd never been on a concrete floor before. I'd never been in this position before.

It was now 3:00 P.M. The same two ladies from before brought our dinner. It was the same as my breakfast and lunch: two sandwiches, one orange, and a frozen drink. But this time, I had 10–15 kernels of popcorn. I was happy for this popcorn. It was a treat, but my spirit began to fade. I'd been locked up in the basement bathroom since 6:00 A.M. It was after 3:00 P.M. now. I knew I wouldn't get arraigned today. I was sitting down and rocking back and forth, trying to keep from crying. I felt if I cried, the Three Stooges from the Buena Vista Police Department would have won. I didn't know how much longer I could hold out As I sat there and rocked, I thought of how cold I was. Eventually, I dozed off to sleep, but when I awakened, I started to hallucinate. I thought rats were coming underneath the cracks of the door, eating away at my feet and working their way up my legs. I jumped up and tried to run toward the door to get away, when one of my cell mates hollered at me as I was getting ready to beat on the door and scream!!!

"You'll be okay, calm down! You can make it. Just think happy thoughts. You can make it."

I lay back down on my mat, and I thought about my PF Flyers that were one of my favorite memories of my childhood, as I would run up and down Ferris Avenue. I believed what the advertisement meant, that when you had on PF Flyers, you had jets on your feet. You could outrun a car; you could fly as high as a plane; a train was no competition for you when you had on PF Flyers. Lord, I wished I had on some now so I could run away from this place, this jail cell that is truly hell.

My second happiest moment was seeing my grandmother, the late Mrs. Lenora Black, riding in a convertible during the Memorial Day parade. She was a Blue Star Mother and president of her chapter, the George Washington Carver History of the Blue Star Mothers of America, Inc.

On January 22, 1942, the *Flint News Advertiser* printed a coupon asking mothers of servicemen to return the coupon after filling it out. The following February 1st, 300 mothers met in the Durant Hotel in Flint, Michigan. Captain George H. Maines, who had conceived the idea for this group, acted as the chair of this first meeting. It was decided that they would form a permanent organization after receiving 1,000 responses from the ad. On February 6th, the organization was reported on congressional record. Chapters then formed in Michigan, Ohio, Wisconsin, New York, Pennsylvania, Oregon, California, Iowa, and Washington. In June of 1960, the organization was chartered by Congress. Mothers volunteered throughout the tough times of World War II. They worked in hospitals, train stations, packed care packages for soldiers, and were a working part of homeland security during times of war. The organization waned in size over the years but has held together by mothers showing pride in both their children and country. In recent times, we have begun to grow in strength. Being attacked on our own soil has once again started mothers hanging flags in their windows at home proclaiming pride in the fact that we have children protecting our freedom during a time of war. Our organization not only provides support for active duty service personnel, promotes patriotism, assists veteran organizations, but also is available to assist in homeland volunteer efforts to help our country remain strong.

I thought about the heaven and hell parties the Blue Star Mothers gave yearly. You would reach into a brown paper bag and pull out a piece of paper, and it would read "heaven" or "hell." Heaven was ice cream and cake with a halo tied around your head. Hell was hot chili. You would go into the basement and dance and sing, "I loved going to hell." I shared with my grandmother how much hell meant to me. She explained to me that hell was a place that I should never want to go to. But, as a youngster, I didn't understand what she was talking about. Hell, to me, meant eating chili and doing the twist. But, at this moment, I understood what my grandmother was speaking about. This was truly hell!!!

As quickly as I started to cry I stopped myself. I felt if I cried, the Three Stooges would have won the battle. I asked the Lord to send my grandmother to me (Lenora Black). I wanted my grandmother to wrap her arms around me and minister to me. I needed love that only a grandmother could provide.

I remembered a man I met in 1981 named Paul Hare. He was a slender, dark-skinned man with a receding hairline, very soft spoken. He always had on jogging attire and running shoes. I met him at Stewart

School. He was watching me play volley ball. He thought I moved quickly. He asked me to join his running club. I said no at first. He returned the following week and asked if he could talk to me for a minute about the joys of running. I thought to myself, he's nuts, but I will talk to him to get him away from me after practice. He told me if I learned to run, nothing could get to me. I would have peace that other people would only dream of. Now, I really knew this man was nuts, but as I listened to him, he made running seem magical. I never did drugs or consumed alcoholic beverages, but he's telling me about a runner's high. This I wanted to check out. I agreed to meet him at Flint Central High School track. It was supposed to be Paul Hare, myself, and three other ladies. The three ladies didn't show. That gave him and me a chance to talk. He asked me if I believed in **GOD**. I said yes. He told me there was a scripture in the Bible he wanted me to learn, to ready myself for the 10-mile run he wanted me to get in shape for. The Bobby Crim Road Race.

The Crim Road Race in 1977 contributed something to the athletes of Michigan Special Olympics. Bobby began organizing this small road race in his home community to establish three main goals. First, to run a world-class road race in the city of Flint, Michigan; second, to raise charitable dollars for mentally handicapped athletes; and finally, to foster community pride and cooperation among the residents of the Greater Flint area. I asked him the scripture. Then I went home to look up Isaiah 40:31: "They that wait upon the **LORD** shall renew [their] strength; they shall mount up with wings as eagles; they shall run, and not be weary; [and] they shall walk, and not faint."

The first time I went on a long run with Paul Hare I felt tired. Paul told me to start quoting the scripture, but I was too tired. I couldn't say it verbally so he started to speak it to me. He also said, "Believe it and achieve; yes, you can do it." Suddenly, I felt as if wings were underneath my arms. My knees began to lift. I was able to finish the run with him. In my first attempt in the Bobby Crim Road Race, I was able to complete it in 84 minutes. Paul would show up at different mile markers to cheer me on. He was at the third-mile marker, telling me to push it. I was looking good at the eighth-mile marker. He showed up again. I was so tired at that point; he encouraged me to lift my legs to finish the race. Always finish what you start he told me. I was in shape and finished strong. Once I crossed the finish line, Paul Hare was there. Again, he told me I didn't need him, that I could do all this again without him, and never give up. I will always remember Paul Hare for encouraging me to run and finish.

I stopped feeling sorry for myself. I'm a Christian and a runner, and now I understand a tactic that Paul Hare used on me. He would tell me to meet him at Flint Central High School track, but that morning, he would call, telling me he's going to be late and for me to run anyway. I would offer to wait for him. "No," he replied, "I want you to run without me. I'll meet you there later." I would run at 9:00 A.M. He would show up about 10:00 A.M. and ask me how my run went.

"Fine," I replied.

He told me I was strong enough to run on my own and never let anyone stop me from my daily run—not him or anyone else. Never allow anyone to take my peace of mind.

At that moment, I started to sing and worship **GOD**. I started singing, "Jesus, You're the Center of My Joy," by Richard Smallwood.

CHORUS

Jesus, you're the center of my joy
All that's good and perfect comes from you
You're the heart of my contentment
Hope for all I do
Jesus, you're the center of my joy

VERSE 1

When I've lost my direction
You're the compass for my way
You're the fire and light
When nights are long and cold
In sadness, you're my laughter
That shatters all my fears
When I'm all alone, your hand is there to hold

I thought of my grandmother's funeral, and I remembered the song "**GOD** Is." I began to sing it so I could feel closer to my grandmother.

"**GOD** Is," by the late Rev. James Cleveland

> God is the joy and the strength of my life,
> He moves all pain, misery, and strife.
> He promised to keep me, never to leave me.
> He's never ever come short of His word.

I was able to fall asleep, and the next thing I heard was someone speaking in a loud masculine voice telling me to wake up. I just lay there for a moment feeling motionless, and he yelled again, "GET UP!!!!" I began to crawl with my eyes closed. I tried to get up. I didn't have the energy to move by myself so one of my cell mates tried to help me get up. I pressed myself against the wall with my eyes closed, trying to walk toward the voice. I couldn't see. It was hard going from pure darkness to light. My eyes were trying to visualize, but I couldn't see where I was going. I tried walking with my eyes closed. I was not responding to the voice. Instead, I was asking what time it was. He answered, "1:30 A.M." I was trying to figure out how long I was in that cold, dark bathroom. I knew they locked me up in there at 6:00 A.M. If it was 1:30 A.M., I had been locked up in that cold, dark bathroom for 19½ hours. After 3:00 P.M., no one came to check on us until 1:30 A.M. So, 10½ hours went by and no one checked in on us. We could have become ill; we could have fought each other. I'll never understand the Saginaw County Jail system. This system is cruel and unjust.

The voice told me and my cell mates to follow him. He took us over to a room to get a thin, gray blanket (full of holes), a white top sheet, very thin, and a new orange mat. He unlocked a door and told us to find a bunk. I asked him to help me. I could not see. My head was spinning, my body was very weak, as though I had no strength. He told me, "I am not going to help you. Find a bunk on your own!!!" My redheaded cell mate pointed me to an upper bunk. I got in and fell back asleep.

Saturday morning I was awakened by a dark-skinned African-American female wearing a short Afro. I tried to ignore her, but she was shaking my arm. Finally, I opened my eyes. "Come on, roomy, you got to eat. Come on, wake up and eat!"

I asked where I was.

She replied, "Saginaw County Jail."

I sat straight up in the bed and looked around. Then I saw a melting pot of women of all races: Caucasian, African-American, Hispanic. I finally jumped down to get my breakfast. I was so happy it wasn't that same breakfast and lunch I had previously of two dry bologna sandwiches and maybe 10 kernels of popcorn. After I finished with my breakfast, I lay back down and fell back asleep. I was awakened by the sound of running water and laughter. I looked around. The ladies were taking showers and brushing their teeth. I remembered a small piece of soap that was handed to me, but I couldn't remember by whom. I wanted to take a shower and brush my teeth, but I didn't have a toothbrush. In walked a female African-American jail guard. I asked, "May I have a toothbrush?"

She replied, "No, you are not at a hotel!!"

I told her, "I don't understand what you are saying."

She replied, "It's like this. You have to have money placed in your account. You place your order on Tuesday, and you receive your merchandise the following Thursday."

I looked at her and said, "I don't have any money, but I would like to brush my teeth." I asked her if I could charge it and pay later. She started laughing and walked out of the cell.

I took my shower with this odorless soap bar that was very small. I tried to rinse my mouth out with water. I looked around for a water fountain, but they didn't have one, so I asked my cell mates, is there a water fountain around here? They laughed and told me "NO!!!"

When I went to the TV room, people there wanted to know what I was in jail for. I told them what happened. A few of the ladies lived in Buena Vista. One asked me, "Was it the big white boy?"

I responded, "Yes!"

She replied, "All he does is stop and harass people and holler at them. Was there a black cop with him?"

I said, "Yes."

She said, "Yes, that's his black sidekick. I know if they stopped you, you didn't do nothing. Buena Vista is one of the dirtiest police forces in the country."

I responded, "Yes, I had heard my co-workers discussing how dirty Buena Vista police were." I shared with her that I didn't know that I was in Buena Vista. I only went that way because of the construction on my regular exit which is the Reese/Caro Exit. I told her I thought to the right was to Buena Vista and to the left was Saginaw. "My co-worker didn't tell me that if I went on Outer Drive, it's Buena Vista. I would not have gone that way otherwise."

She said, "You will be okay and be able to beat the bogus rap sheet."

We played cards all day until 11:00 P.M., which was bedtime. Sunday morning, I kept hearing about shakedown Sunday where the guards come and search your belongings and go through your bunks to see if you are hiding food or weapons. They also shared with me that we must remove our clothing and wrap ourselves in a towel and wait for our clothing to be washed and brought back to us. When I heard this I prayed. It was cold in here. I couldn't imagine being wrapped in a damp towel for an extended period of time. I asked GOD to please spare me from shakedown Sunday.

Saturday we did the same thing as the day before: watched TV and played cards till around 8:00 P.M. Then the door opened with two jail guards carrying new, clean, hot, out-of-the dryer jail clothing. I **THANKED GOD**. It felt good to step into some warm clothing. After the jail guards left, one of my cell mates called me and asked me to stand in the middle of the room. She had all of the other cell mates to make a circle around me. She started praying. I started weeping. The people that I thought were no good were praying for me: the crackheads, thieves, meth heads, and alcoholics were praying for me. I was overcome with emotion.

Monday morning, October 2, 2006, I ate breakfast at 5:00 A.M. I noticed a new Caucasian lady sleeping across from me with long blond hair. A few hours later, they called my name and the other lady's too, which I thought was odd. She came in Sunday night after we went to bed, and she's being arraigned with me after I arrived at 12:30 A.M.

Friday morning, and I was not being arraigned until Monday morning 9:00 A.M. I smelled a rat. I was almost 100 percent certain the big Caucasian cop made the African-American cop hold up my paperwork since they didn't care that I was on my way to work. They were trying to force me to miss as many days from work as possible, especially since the black cop said he didn't care about me or my job. They were trying to get me fired.

We followed the jail guard back to the holding cell where I was first placed. There was a plus-size African-American female snoring extremely loud there. We stood there for 5 minutes, then a Caucasian male with blue pants, blue shirt, and tie woke her up and told her to plead guilty and she would be okay. She looked up at him and told him all right.

As soon as he closed the door, I asked her what was she pleading guilty to. As soon as she tried to answer me, a female guard entered and told us to be quiet. I tried to walk behind the young lady and ask her again, but once more, the female guard yelled, **"DIDN'T I TELL YOU TO BE QUIET???"**

Once we entered the room where I was being arraigned, I looked around, and to my surprise, there were nothing but 25 African-American males, one Caucasian male, two African-American females (which included me), and one Caucasian female. I wondered how many African-American males were there on bogus charges like I was. I thought to myself, *This is nothing but a form of slavery; instead of having us work on the plantation, they put us in jail.*

I listened as they called a few people to be arraigned, and none of them had money to hire a lawyer. I felt so saddened by this situation. Finally, it was my turn. The Caucasian judge told me of the charges against me and asked how I pleaded. I told him I did nothing. He asked again, "How do you plea, guilty or not guilty?"

I answered, "I did nothing!!"

He said, "Then you are pleading not guilty."

I replied, "I did nothing, Your Honor."

He said, "Your bail is set at $5,000," then he went down to $3,000, and then down to $1,500. Then he asked if I was going to use a public defender or hire a lawyer. I told him I would be hiring a lawyer. He looked at me strangely because everyone before me was using a public defender. I turned to the Michigan state police officer who was seated to my right, and I asked, "Is this over?"

He started laughing and said, "You need $150, and then you can go home."

I asked him, "How do I make a telephone call?"

He told me to talk to the male deputy sheriff that was at the back of the room, so I walked toward him and asked him if he would take me to a telephone. I explained my inmate numbers hadn't been activated. He told me to tell the female jail guard when I got back downstairs. **GUESS WHO WAS STANDING THERE?** The mean, evil jail guard I affectionately named Wicked Wanda, the jail guard from when I was locked up in the bathroom. She said, "I have your paperwork in my hand."

I asked her to take me to a telephone so I could make a call to get my bail money. She replied, "NO!!! With all those charges you got on you, **YOU AIN'T GOING NOWHERE.**"

I said, "Here's my paperwork. I need $150 and I can go home; plus, I have to go to work tonight."

She replied, **"GET YOUR ASS IN THERE AND SIT DOWN. YOU SHOULD HAVE ASKED THE JUDGE FOR WORK RELEASE. YOU AIN'T GOING NOWHERE. GET IN THERE!!!"**

I walked back into my cell. My roommates asked me what happened. I told them Wicked Wanda wouldn't take me to make a call. They read over my paperwork. They said, "You can leave. What's wrong with her?" They told me to wait until 6:00 P.M. and maybe the guard will let me use the telephone.

I went back to the card table and started playing cards. Then Wicked Wanda opened up the door she told me some man called for me. I asked who it was. She answered that she didn't know and she didn't care. She had a white sheet of notebook paper in her hand. She threw it at me and told me tomorrow was Tuesday and it was visiting day and she was working and if anybody was coming to visit me and their name was not on that sheet of paper, she wasn't going to let me see them, and then she walked out and slammed the door.

We were gambling for an orange after playing cards. Then we started to watch the soap opera *One Life to Live* around 2:59 P.M. The door opened and guess who entered the room.

Wicked Wanda.

I couldn't make out what she was saying. I heard my cell mates calling my name. I replied, "Yeah, what's up?"

They were jumping up and down. **"YOU CAN GO!!!!!"**

"Go where?" I asked.

"Home, Home, Home!"

I didn't understand. Wicked Wanda was standing there not saying anything. Then she said, "You can roll up." I didn't have a clue as to what that meant. The women were telling me to go and get the sheets, blanket, and my towel and roll them up. I did as they told me, and they all lined up at the door to tell me good-bye and good luck with my case.

I followed Wicked Wanda to a room, then she pointed at a plastic bag. I opened it. It was my clothing. I changed into my street clothes. **GOD** is such a good **GOD**. I had to hold my tongue. I wanted to say to Wicked Wanda, "I thought you said I wasn't going anywhere." I followed her back to the area where I first came in. Two African-American males were standing there. An older gentleman about 60 who looked to be around 6 foot 4, 200 pounds, and wearing glasses was one of them. The younger male also wore glasses. He stood around 5 foot 11 and weighed about 195 pounds. The older man knew my uncle Michael. They asked why I didn't call home. They had been sending me messages. I told them I never received them. I glanced to my left and Wicked Wanda was standing there amazed that we were engaging in conversation.

She prejudged me by my charges, not realizing that police can lie and demean someone's character. Not all police officers are honest. Hopefully, she learned to treat people with respect and dignity that day, and not go by what's on a police report. She stood there the whole time while they talked to me with her arms folded and a solemn look on her face. I placed my hand over my mouth as they were talking to me because I hadn't brushed my teeth in 4 days!! They asked me why I was there. I answered and said because of a Buena Vista police officer who was a liar and an idiot. They started to laugh and said, "Oh, you came to jail 'cause you hurt their feelings."

They told me my mother had been there and posted my bail at 12:06 p.m. I said, "It's after 3:00 p.m. Why did it take so long for me to be released?"

They answered, "The Buena Vista chief of police, Brian Booker, took his time about signing the paperwork. We couldn't release you until he signed the release form." It was only a 10-minute ride for him. I couldn't understand why it took him 3 hours to arrive.

Buena Vista is truly a den of snakes. Now I understand why the three officers acted dirty. They emulate their leader's actions. If it takes him 3 hours to sign a paper to release me after my bail was paid, what kind of people are they? The deputy sheriff told me to go outside, someone was waiting for me. "Who is it?" I asked.

They said, "If you told an officer he was a liar and an idiot, I know you aren't scared to go out that door!!"

I started laughing and asked what he looked like. Just so I would know I was going with the right man. He replied, "You bad; go on out the door." Then they asked if they stopped me, would I call them an idiot? I responded, "Yes, if you stop me for bogus reasons, as they did, yes, I will." They both laughed and told me good luck with my case

I walked out the door and there's only one man out there named Zoe. I asked, "Are you the man that I am supposed to go with?" He said yes. I said, "Okay, I have no choice." He told that he knew my aunt from working with her at Moon's Funeral Home in Flint. I said okay. He was well dressed and well mannered.

He drove me over to Buena Vista Police Department. The young lady working behind the desk refused to allow me to do the paperwork because I didn't have any ID. I tried to explain to her my purse was locked up in the trunk of my car so Zoe had to do the paperwork for me. She released all the information to him. Then we drove to pick up my car in Bridgeport, Michigan (Gobeyn's Marathon).

I saw the tow truck driver. He was working. I stared at him hard to see if he remembered me. He acted as though he didn't. He gave Zoe a pink slip of paper. We then drove to another location to pick up my vehicle. Upon arriving, Zoe entered a small white building. During this time, I began to observe all the vehicles that were on the property, and I began to wonder if these cars were there from harassment by the Buena

Vista Police Department. Once Zoe returned, I thanked him for all he had done. I told him he was my guardian angel.

During my drive home, I turned on the radio. The song playing was by the late Luther Vandross, **"SHINE."** The song states you're going to get your time to shine, and that song represented to me all the darkness and lies that I had encountered. Eventually, I would have my day in court, and that day I will **SHINE!!!**

Upon my arrival home, I jumped into the shower and finally brushed my teeth. I immediately called my supervisor QB. I left him a voice mail to explain why I hadn't been to work in 2 days. I asked for this day off so that I could sleep in my bed, but if he needed me to report to work, to call me on my cell and I'll be there.

After I relaxed for around an hour or so, Zoe called. He had a lawyer he wanted me to use and said that he would be calling me back when he found out what judge would hear my case. I asked his name. "Thomas Frank," he replied. He assured me this man was good. He told me he would call back as soon as he found out. His son was a judge. He wanted to make sure that his son wouldn't be hearing my case since that would be a conflict of interest. I fell to my knees, and I started praying to **GOD** that if Thomas Frank was the man he wanted me use, to give me a sign!!! Zoe had done so much for me, and I felt as though he was my guardian angel. I asked the Lord to give me the strength to make the right decision.

The telephone rang. It was my mother. She had cooked me a gorgeous meal of baked chicken, yams, mac and cheese, corn bread, and greens, and for dessert, her famous "German Chocolate Cake." I couldn't wait to get there.

Once I arrived, we had dinner. She wanted to know what took me so long to get out of jail. She paid my bail at 12:06 P.M. They released me at 3:05 P.M. I explained to her that the chief of police from Buena Vista (Brian Booker) had to sign a document in order for me to be released. I replied that it was only a 10-minute drive from the Buena Vista Police Department to the Saginaw County Jail. She became upset about the time frame after I explained it to her.

"The people at the Buena Vista Police Department are criminals. They don't care how long I had to wait or the fact that I am a law-abiding citizen THAT DID NO WRONG!!!"

She asked me what happened to me that night. After I explained to her what happened, she was ready to fight!!! She told me when Tonnie J called and told her I was in jail, she sat straight up in the bed!!! She couldn't understand what I could have done. She had talked to me at 9:00 P.M. that night, and I sounded like my usual self, so it was hard for her to understand how I became inmate #140409. Then when she called to find out the charges and she had to say *inmate,* that made her cry. She said, Friday, one of her sisters told her to call Judge P, who is a member of the same church I attend, to see if he could help in my release. Saturday, she spent the day praying and crying with my friend Tonnie J. I asked her, "You two spent Saturday crying and praying?" Yes, she answered. I started laughing. "Mom, I was fine. **GOD** blessed me to be locked up with kind, compassionate women. Mom, they prayed for me; they cheered for me when I was released. I can't say anything bad about the ladies **GOD** had surrounded me with. They took wonderful care of me. I can talk about the jail guards and the police, the people that are paid to protect me. They are the people that wronged me."

She stared at me for a moment. She wanted to know what they were arrested for. I explained, "Mom, I told you, they were thieves, crackheads, meth heads, but they were good to me. We all are **GOD'S** children." I started to laugh. "The police from Buena Vista are Satan's children." She laughed too.

She explained to me about Sunday morning when she went to GEBC for a baptism service with her goddaughter Arlene, whose youngest son was being baptized. Arlene is also one of my best friends. She shared with me how Judge P walked up to her before service and told her there wasn't anything he could do for me. "She needs a lawyer," and then he walked away coldly, as if he believed the charges. She became upset, but Arlene consoled her.

I told her, "Don't be upset. He's a judge. Naturally he's going to believe the charges, so forgive him." She told me when LB was singing "My Soul Has Been Anchored" with the lyrics by Douglas Miller, how comforting that was to her.

Though the storms keep on raging in my life,
And sometimes it's hard to tell the night from day.

Still that hope that lies within is reassured
As I keep my eyes upon the distant shore;
I know He'll lead me safely to that blessed place He has prepared
But if the storms don't cease,
And if the wind keeps on blowing [in my life]
My soul has been anchored in the Lord.

I told her that I felt sorry for what she had to endure from the actions of a Caucasian, racist, sexist officer and an African-American sellout officer that allowed the Caucasian officer to instruct him to take me to jail, knowing that I had committed no crime. What really saddens me about this situation is that he comes from the womb of an African-American woman. He's aware of the injustices that our people have suffered through history, then he turns around and he's doing the same thing that the Caucasian man has been doing to us for years. When do we get the same rights as everyone else? They would not have stopped a Caucasian woman and treated her in the manner I was treated, and this African-American officer has a mother, sister, aunt, and cousin, and maybe a wife. Would he want any of them to be treated in this manner? Of course, not!!

"But, Mom, I'll tell you this. I am going to fight them until I can't fight anymore. I am in this for the long haul!!!"

My mother asked me, "Are you going to call your pastor?"

"NO," I replied!!!

She asked why not. I answered, "He's not concerned about me."

She then asked, "Why do you feel that way?"

I answered, "Mom, I'm a blue-collar worker. He's more concerned for the doctors, lawyers, judges, educators, those types of people. I work on the assembly line for General Motors and that's not enough to make him support my injustice."

"Kim, if you feel that way, why are you a member of that church?"

I answered, "Because of the strong love I have for my grandmother, Lenora Black. I heard her praying in that church. I heard her singing, 'Oh, how I love Jesus,' and I watched her working on the food committee. She was a deaconess. I bowled with her on the first church bowling league in 1979 at the now-closed Dort Bowling Center located on

S. Dort Highway. Her funeral was at that church. I survived in jail by singing **'GOD IS,'** which was a song at her funeral. I only stayed for those memories and the memories of growing up under the leadership of the late Pastor Emeritus Brady; no other reason. Mom, when I was in jail, I asked the Lord to send her to me. That's the only way I could survive."

My mother stared at me for a few minutes and asked, "You didn't want me?"

I explained to her, "My grandmother was what I needed at that time, no disrespect to you."

She asked me had I given any thoughts to a lawyer. "Yes," I answered, "Zoe has a lawyer he wants me to use." She asked if it was the man in the cowboy attire she met on the elevator with Zoe. I replied, "I don't know. All I know is that the man he wants me to use is the lawyer he used prior. The lawyer's son is a judge. Zoe is making some calls to see what judge I will go before. If I don't go before his son, then he wants me to use this lawyer named Thomas Frank."

She asked me if I trusted someone out of Saginaw. "I trust Zoe. When a man can help me without knowing me, I trust that **GOD** sent him in my life for a reason. Once he dropped me off in Bridgeport to pick up my car that could have been the end of it, but, no. He's still working it out for me. I trust and believe **GOD!!!**"

As I readied myself to leave, my mom asked if I was going to work tonight. I answered, no, that I called my boss, and I explained my situation to him and requested the night off. She told me she went to my job Sunday night and left a letter for him at the front gate, explaining to him that I was missing from work due to a situation I had no control over. After that, I got a piece of German chocolate cake to take home. Mom followed me outside to look at the light over my license plate. I started my car, and she saw it working. I told her, "Mom, I have a lot of people I owe apologies to."

"Why?" she asked.

I said I never believed in driving while black. I thought people were lying when they said they were just driving down the street and were stopped and harassed by the police, and it's a terrible thing to say, but I'd rather sit down and eat dinner with my cell mates that were in jail for drugs and stealing, than having dinner with a lying, low-down police officer from Buena Vista. They took away my rights to be on a jury. I would never believe the evidence they provided. I have no trust in a police officer at this time.

"Mom, thank you very much for all your support and for believing in me."

On my drive home, I thought about some of the poetry and quotes my father has in his house.

"Believe in the strength of your spirit. The power of your purpose. The dignity of your dream."

—*Betty Shabazz*

"The ultimate measure of a man is not where he stands in moments of comfort and convenience, but where he stands at times of challenge and controversy."

—*Martin Luther King, Jr.*

"Corruption runs in high places!"

—*The late Frederick George Sampson . . . pastor of Tabernacle Missionary Baptist Church, Detroit, Michigan*

I didn't quite understand what Pastor Sampson meant when he said police have their hands on almost everything dealing with corruption. The church said "Amen" and clapped. Now I wish he was alive so I could go to him and tell him, "I UNDERSTAND EVERYTHING YOU SAID THAT SUNDAY!!"

Once I got home I called a few of my male friends that had shared with me how they were stopped and harassed by Mount Morris Police and Grand Blanc Police. I shared my experience with them. They couldn't believe me, being a female, that they took me to jail. I said, "Yes, they get sisters too."

The next night, I was traveling to my job. I was approaching the Holland Road Exit, and my stomach had butterflies in it. I started to sweat. I started to hyperventilate. I had never suffered anxiety attacks before. I kept driving. I started praying until I exited off the Reese/Caro Exit which is under construction. That's my usual exit. I just have to deal with the construction. I cannot go down Outer Drive **AGAIN!!!**

When I took my lunch to the break area, my co-worker was waiting with paperwork. My boss was on sick leave, but he left me paperwork so that I could be excused for the days off of work. We had our usual meeting before we started working, then one of my co-workers asked me what happened to me. I was supposed to bring him a fish dinner from Woods Barbeque that night. I told him I had it, but I went to jail instead. Everyone turned and looked at me in disbelief. He really didn't believe me I told them I was not making a joke about this. **I HAD BEEN IN JAIL!!!!** Of course, they wanted to know why. I shared with them why, and I let them know I was on Outer Drive. They started laughing at me. A co-worker said everybody knows not to go on Outer Drive. Well, I didn't. I wish someone would have shared that with me.

My next night at work during break, I noticed my co-workers staring at me. I asked them what's going on. They pointed to a picture of a female with two black eyes. Underneath the picture they wrote "Kim's mug shot" and started laughing, so I started laughing too . . . so I wouldn't cry.

October 4, 2006, 9:00 A.M., the lawyer Zoe wanted me to hire called. He would meet me October 6th at 10:00 A.M., in M. T. Thompson Jr.'s courtroom #306.

The next night at work as I was walking, one of my co-workers stopped me, questioning me about what happened to me. I shared with him my situation. He told me, **"FIGHT BACK!!!!"** He shared Buena Vista was a corrupt, low-down, dirty police force, and someone needed to stand up to them. The people in Buena Vista act as if they are scared of them. Someone needs to take them down. I gave him a thumbs-up. I replied, "I am in it to win it!!!!"

He asked me if one of them was the big white boy. I said yes. He asked, "Was there a black guy with him?"

"Yes," I replied.

He said, "That's what I thought. They're dirty. **FIGHT THEM BACK!!!**"

We hugged and said our good-byes.

The morning of October 6th, 8:00 A.M., my shift ended. I walked to the locker room to shower and change clothes. As I was walking, my co-workers were giving me the thumbs-up, telling me they have my back.

Police, Lawyers & Judges

If I needed them they will be willing to testify about my character. That was a wonderful feeling to know that many love you.

After my shower and change of clothes, on my drive to the courthouse, I prayed and asked GOD to give me strength for the task before me as I entered courtroom #306. I sat down in the back of the courtroom waiting for my lawyer in the jury box. One of my cell mates, the redheaded one that was locked up in the bathroom with me, was there. A man was seated next to her. We waved at each other. I asked her to tell everyone hello for me. I noticed the judge watching us communicate back and forth. Judge M. T. Thompson Jr. (African-American), with a dark brown complexion, had on black glasses. He appeared to be short, maybe 5 foot 6 or 5 foot 7. He looked to be around 55–63 years old. He gave me a look for me to stop communicating with my ex-cell mate.

The prosecutor appeared and started reading the charges against her and her brother. Her brother was baldheaded; he had such an evil demeanor on his face. Once I started hearing the charges on them I couldn't believe it!! Her brother had broken out of some law facility in Lake Orion. She was so kind to me during the time I was locked up in the bathroom. She's the one that helped me up when I couldn't get myself together. This was her third offense. She started to cry. I started crying with her. She had a 15-year-old son. I wondered what was going to happen to him. She and her brother were removed from the courtroom.

In walked my lawyer. He's Caucasian, maybe around 62 years old. He was dressed in cowboy attire, even cowboy boots. He was slender, maybe 6 foot or 6 foot 1. He had a thin gray ponytail that hung midway down his back. He could have been a hippie back in the day. We smiled and shook hands and waited for my name to be called, which took around 15 minutes. Once my name was called, we walked up front and took our seats at the table. As we sat there, no one from the prosecutor's office or the Buena Vista Police Department showed up. My attorney asked for the police reports. Judge Thompson Jr. told him there weren't any. My attorney jumped up and walked to my right and started speaking in a loud tone that he was there, I was here, and what's the problem with the police and prosecutor? Where are the police reports?? They had had one week to get it together.

Judge Thompson Jr. replied he will make sure that he receives the paperwork he was requesting. My attorney looked over at the court reporter and asked her if she had anything. She replied, "NO, that's not my job."

We left. As we were walking out, he asked me what happened. I told him my story again. He replied, "Something's going on, and I will get to the bottom of it. How are they charging you?" he asked. "With fleeing and eluding without a speeding ticket?"

I smiled. I told him, "You will find out I'm innocent of all charges."

October 13, 2006. 10:00 A.M. I had another appointment in Judge Thompson Jr.'s courtroom #306. This time I was accompanied by my mother. We sat in the courtroom. Then she turned to me and said, "Kim, the judge is no good. I can look at him and tell."

I replied, "Mom, give him a chance to prove himself." My attorney had paperwork in his hand and motioned for me to follow him outside of the courtroom to read the police reports.

Buena Vista Twp. Police Department, SUPPLEMENTAL Incident REPORT 0001
ORIGINAL DATE INCIDENT
Thu, Sep 28, 2006, 856-0001897-06 NO
SUPPLEMENTARY DATE FILE CLASS
Fri, Sep 29, 2006 54003
INCIDENT STATUS: Open
I. FLEEING & ELUDING/R&O STATE/POSSESSION OF OC SPRAY
INFORMATION:

I was dispatched to Fuller St. and S. Outer St. for a female search. Upon arrival, I met with Officer Douglas who asked me to search his female suspect. Suspect, Kim Rose, was seated and handcuffed in the back of the patrol vehicle. I opened the vehicle door and asked the suspect to exit the vehicle, sliding her feet out first. She replied, "What the hell do you want?" I then reached into the patrol vehicle and helped the suspect out of the vehicle. As I pulled her out of the vehicle, she started pulling away from me and started calling me names.

He said, "What the hell do you want, you stupid bitch?" As I was conducting my search, she tried pulling away from me a second time. During my search, I found a can of animal deterrent spray in her right front sweatshirt pocket. After my search I secured Rose back.

ARREST:
NAME: KIM R. DAVIS
CHARGE: 8177 POLICE OFFICER–FLEEING 3RD DEGREE VEHICLE CODE 257.602a(3)
Status: Open
Buena Vista Twp. Police Department
ORIGINAL INCIDENT REPORT
ORIGINAL DATE: Thu, Sep 28, 2006
INCIDENT NO.: 856-0001897-06(10)
TIME RECEIVED: 2348
FILE CLASS: 54003
WORK UNIT PD BUENA VISTA TWP COUNTY: SAGINAW
COMPLAINANT PATROL TELEPHONE NO
ADDRESS: 3438
STREET: Genei Avenue
CITY: Saginaw
STATE: Michigan
ZIP CODE: 48601
INCIDENT STATUS: Open
FLEEING & ELUDING/R&O STATE/POSSESSION OF OC

SUMMARY:

R/O was traveling N/B on Outer Dr. near Lapeer when I observed suspect's vehicle traveling in the same direction with the registration light out. R/O followed the suspect's vehicle and observed the vehicle swerve to the east side of the roadway crossing the fog line. R/O activated emergency lights and observed suspect's vehicle slow down and pull to the east side of the road, appearing to pull over at N. Outer and Wadsworth. The suspect's vehicle did not come to a complete stop. R/O then observed the suspect's vehicle pull back onto the roadway and continue driving N/B on Outer Dr. R/O then turned on sirens and suspect continued going N/B on Outer Dr., at which point R/O notified SCCD that I had a vehicle going N/B on Outer Dr. near Wadsworth that was slow to stop. The suspect's vehicle continued N/B on Outer Dr., passing Irving, Monmouth, Exeter, Sears, North, and Norman. Officer Patterson got involved in the pursuit at North Street. Officer Patterson also activated his lights and sirens.

The suspect's vehicle finally stopped just north of Fuller. R/O exited the patrol vehicle and ordered the suspect to step out of her vehicle. The suspect refused to step out of her vehicle. She was sitting in the driver seat with her hands on the steering wheel, in a blank stare. R/O walked up to the vehicle and opened the driver-side door, at which point Officer Patterson walked over to the passenger-side door. R/O ordered the suspect to step out of the vehicle, at which point the suspect got out of the, moving, her hands around in front of my face. R/O asked the suspect had she been drinking. The suspect replied "no." R/O then asked the suspect why she continued on after I activated lights and sirens. The suspect stated, "I was not going to pull over on a dark road." (All streetlights were working; the road was well lit.) The suspect further stated that she was going to pull into the gas station up the street. R/O ordered the suspect to put her hands on the side of the vehicle, at which point the suspect stated, "Y'all didn't have anything better to do than to pull me over!" Suspect was very uncooperative. R/O then ordered the suspect to step to the back of the vehicle and put her hands on the trunk. The suspect put her hands on the trunk, then she moved her left hand toward her pocket. R/O ordered the suspect to keep her hands on the vehicle, at which point the suspect turned around, removing both of her hands off the vehicle and faced R/O. Suspect then became verbally aggressive. R/O ordered the suspect to turn around and place her hands on the back of the vehicle. Suspect refused to turn around and place her hands on the vehicle, at which point R/O attempted to physically turn the suspect around. R/O reached toward the suspect in an attempt to place her back on the vehicle, at which point the suspect pushed R/O's hand away and stated, "I will whoop your ass." R/O then proceeded to handcuff the suspect and place her under arrest, at which point the suspect pulled away. R/O then grabbed the suspect's arm and placed it behind her back, at which point she was handcuffed. The suspect was then placed in the back of R/O's patrol vehicle. The suspect continued to swear at officers calling them "bitches" and "motherfuckers."

PAGE
1 of 3
INVESTIGATED BY OFFICER JOSE DOUGLAS #36
REPORTED BY
REVIEWED BY
Buena Vista Twp. Police Department
ORIGINAL INCIDENT
ORIGINAL DATE: Thu, Sep 28, 2006
INCIDENT NO.: 856-0001897-06(10)
TIME RECEIVED: 2348
FILE CLASS: 54003

Officer Villanueva and Sgt. Baker responded to the scene. The suspect called Sgt. Baker a "dirty bitch" and "asshole." Officer Villanueva was asked to search the suspect. Upon searching the suspect, Officer Villanueva found a can of animal deterrent spray in the right front sweatshirt pocket of the suspect. R/O searched the suspect's vehicle and found nothing. The suspect was issued a citation for defective equipment (no registration light). The animal deterrent spray was placed on evidence. The suspect's vehicle was towed by Gobeyn's and the suspect was transported to the Saginaw County Jail where she was lodged for R and O (state) and flee/elude.

While en route to the Saginaw County Jail, the suspect called me a "bitch" and stated, "When I catch you out somewhere, I'm going to whoop your ass."

VENUE:
SAGINAW COUNTY, BUENA VISTA TWP
HOLLAND
AT OR NEAR: 1-675
DATE & TIME: THU, SEP 28, 2006 AT 2348
COMPLAINANT:
NAME: PATROL

NBR: 3438 DIR:
SFX: AVENUE
CTY: SAGINAW
ST: MI
ZIP: 485601
TXH:
TXW:
LIEN/SOS CHECK:
Suspect was clear and valid with no wants.
SUSPECT VEHICLE: White 2005 Pontiac Grand Prix 4-door
Plate #: 3DLH43
VIN #: 2G2WR544551151023
PAGE 2 of 3 INVESTIGATED BY OFFICER CRJ DOUGLAS #36
REPORTED BY REVIEWED BY: Buena Vista Twp. Police Department
ORIGINAL INCIDENT REPORT:
SUSPECT VEHICLE DISPOSITION: Towed by Gobeyn's
ARREST:
RAC: B
SEX: F
DOB:
HGT:
WGT:
HAI:
EYE:
NAM: KIM R. DAVIS
TXW:
CHARGE: 8177 POLICE OFFICER-FLEEING 3RD DEGREE VEHICLE CODE 257.602 a(3)
LODGED: SAGINAW COUNTY JAIL
EXTERNAL DOCUMENTS:
2 supplemental reports
Subject resistance form
Subject in jail form
Saginaw County Jail intake form

Tow card
Evidence sheet
STATUS: Open.
PAGE INVESTIGATED BY OFFICER CR J DOUGLAS #36 REPORTED BY REVIEWED BY: Buena Vista Twp. Police Department Evidence Manager
PROPERTY REPORT
File No.: 06-0001897
Cont. No.:
Charges: Traffic
Investigator: #36 Officer Jose Douglas
Date In: 09/28/2006
Concluded: 09/29/2006
Item Description Current Location Member 0001 3.5 02 can of animal deterrent spray Officer Jose Douglas
Locker A
Buena Vista Twp. Police Department, SUPPLEMENTAL INCIDENT REPORT 0002
INCIDENT STATUS: Open
ORIGINAL DATE: Thu, Sep 28, 2006
SUPPLEMENTARY DATE: Thu, Sep 28, 2006
INCIDENT NO: 856-0001897-06
ITI FILE CLASS: 54003
FLEEING & ELUDING/R&O STATE/POSSESSION OF OC SPRAY
INFORMATION:

While on patrol, this officer was traveling SIB Outer from Washington, when Office Douglas advised Central Dispatch that he had a vehicle refusing to stop. Office Douglas was NIB on Outer, and this officer was able to see his patrol vehicle overhead lights.

This officer immediately drove toward Officer Douglas and pulled over on Outer at North as Officer Douglas approached. Once Officer Douglas and the subject vehicle passed by this officer's location, this officer activated my patrol vehicle's emergency lights and siren and followed behind Officer Douglas.

Once the subject vehicle came up to Outer and Fuller, the subject vehicle pulled into a driveway and stopped. At this time, officer exited the patrol vehicle and approached the subject vehicle. Officer Douglas approached from the driver's side and this officer from the passenger side. Once officers were at the rear of the vehicle, the driver, a BIF, exited the vehicle and instantly became verbally aggressive to Officer Douglas, and then to this officer.

Officer Douglas instructed the BIF to move to the rear of her vehicle and out of the roadway. She continued to be aggressive and verbal toward officers. This officer was able to obtain a picture work ID from the driver and also her birth date.

This officer returned to Officer Douglas's patrol vehicle to conduct a LIEN check on the subject. As this officer was attempting to complete the LIEN check, this officer heard the B/F say to Officer Douglas, "I'll whoop your ass." This officer clearly heard this from within the patrol vehicle. This officer exited the patrol vehicle and returned to Officer Douglas and the BIF subject. Officer Douglas handcuffed the subject and placed her in the rear of the patrol vehicle.

Once Officer Villanueva arrived on scene, the subject was removed from the vehicle to be searched. Once the BIF was outside the vehicle as Officer Villanueva was searching her, the subject attempted to pull away from Officer Villanueva and this officer took control of the BIF subject's arm and secured her up against the patrol vehicle. As Officer Villanueva continued her search, the BIF subject attempted to push away from the vehicle as this officer was trying to control her. Once Officer Villanueva had completed her search, the B/F subject was placed back in the rear of Officer Douglas's patrol vehicle.

This officer stood by with Officer Douglas until Gobeyn's had arrived to take possession of the subject's vehicle.

ARREST:
Name: Kim Davis
Investigated By:
Reported BY:
Reviewed BY:
OFFICER PATTERSON #25

I read the reports. I told him he had the wrong paperwork, that none of this happened. There was so much profanity and lies. He asked, "Isn't this your name at the top?"

"Yes, but none of this happened."

Then I thought, *Get the video*. He asked me, "Did you see a video?"

I answered, "No, but they have them on TV cop shows, after the Rodney King incident. I thought all police forces were made to have them in their cruisers."

"Not Buena Vista," he replied.

I said, "This is how Buena Vista is keeping my people in slavery. They write up lies on their police reports, put all these ridicules charges on my people and myself. Isn't there a state law where all cruisers should have videos?"

Now I was upset. They picked the wrong AFRICAN-AMERICAN WOMAN. I will survive as long as I have GOD on my side. I WILL survive.

My lawyer was silent. We walked back inside. I took my seat next to my mother. I noticed a short Caucasian male with a white shirt, blue tie, and dark blue or black slacks, with dark hair. He was around 5 foot 7 and 5 foot 9. He beckoned to my attorney to go to a room off to the side of the courtroom. Once my attorney reappeared, he motioned for me to follow him outside of the courtroom. My mom and I followed him out. He told me Prosecutor Borchard is offering me a plea of 6 months' probation and misdemeanor on my record for 1 year, but before I could answer, my mother said "NO!!! She didn't do it. She's fighting these charges."

He looked at me for my answer. I told him, "She speaks for both of us." We reentered the courtroom. Judge Thompson Jr. called my name. We took our seat at the table. Prosecutor Borchard jumped up and told Judge Thompson Jr. that he could dismiss this case, and that I was going to take the plea. My attorney immediately stood and told the judge, "No, she's not. She wants her day in court."

I heard my whole name called, including my middle name. I looked to my left. Prosecutor Borchard was telling me if I don't want that plea, he will come after me and he will bring back more charges. He walked to the African-American police officer and hollered, "Give me

SOMETHING ON HER!!!!! Was she speeding? **ANYTHING, ANYTHING!! I WANT HER!!! AND I WILL GET HER!!!!"** He took his pen, looking directly at me, and hitting the yellow notepad, said, **"I WILL GET YOU!!!!"**

My attorney told me to get up and walk out. I looked at Judge Thompson Jr. to see if he was going to tell this man to STOP!! He was just sitting there, watching, as if it were a movie. I walked out backward with my eyes on Prosecutor James T. Borchard, making sure he knew I wasn't afraid. My mother had her purse ready to hit him. My attorney had to go back inside the courtroom to get some paperwork and told me to wait downstairs for him.

Once we got to the elevators, an African-American male who was dark skinned, neat, with a short haircut, wearing a white crispy shirt and blue pants, and who was walking with a cane, came by. He had brown tinted glasses, was around 5 foot 10, and weighed 220 pounds.

Once we entered the elevator, Jose Douglas appeared. He was my arresting officer. He looked unkempt. He was wearing some old tan corduroys and a cream sweater that looked around 10–15 years old. He wouldn't get in the elevator with us. The man with us started talking about Jose Douglas. He said he acted like he hated his own people. I asked him, "Are you here because of Douglas?"

He said, "Yes, that man needs help. All he does is go around calling African-American people 'crackheads.'"

I started jumping up and down. "I'm here because of Douglas." I shared my story with him. He said Douglas is going to fool around and get killed. I said, "Don't be too hard on him. He's trying to fit in with the Caucasian police officer."

He said, "Yes, he's a trip too."

Once off the elevator, we wished each other good luck against Douglas.

My attorney stepped off the elevator and handed me my copy of the police reports. I was anxious to find out the Caucasian's police officer's name, which was Timothy W. Patterson. My attorney told me he's going over to talk to the Buena Vista chief of police to check on the officer with the rape charge. He said, "Kim, you had every right to fear for your safety. He's a personal friend of mine. I don't appreciate what happened to you in the courtroom. Of all my years of practicing law, I never witnessed anything like this. Buena Vista needs to stop what they are doing!! I have another case similar to yours, and I am tired of this." He told me he would call me later.

October 14, 2006. I had to go to my bowling league, which begins at 3:00 P.M. Before bowling, my aunt and uncle walked up to me, wanting to know what happened. I told them I was unjustly stopped, and I had a slight argument with a Caucasian officer. I called him an asshole and a liar. They both walked away before I could tell them how awful I was treated in jail and how I was called a crackhead and slammed into a police cruiser. I tried to concentrate on bowling, but I couldn't. I kept thinking of Prosecutor James T. Borchard who threatened me in the courtroom.

My teammates tried to get me to snap out of it. People don't understand that I have people trying to destroy my life and that's bigger than bowling.

On October 18, 2006, I received a letter from the State of Michigan letting me know that my car was going to be sold by October 27, 2006, for abandonment. I couldn't believe what I was reading. These lowdown Buena Vista police officers were still messing with me!! I called my mother to vent to her. She told me to call my lawyer. I did. I faxed him the paperwork. He said he would take care of everything for me.

On October 30, 2006, the Buena Vista Police Department dropped all of my charges except the charge of defective equipment on my car, which was the light over my license plate.

November 1, 2006. I received paperwork that Prosecutor James T. Borchard was bringing the charges back: fleeing and eluding, resisting and obstructing a police officer. I called my attorney to see if what I was reading was true. He said yes. I asked how the charges could be reissued once they were dropped. He replied, "Prosecutor James T. Borchard has more power than the police." He told me not to worry; he was going to take care of everything.

November 9, 2006. I took a seat in Judge Thompson Jr.'s courtroom #306. A Caucasian young man sat down next to me, sharing his dilemma with a Prosecutor James T. Borchard. He forgot to show up for his appointment, and Prosecutor James T. Borchard was trying to throw the book at him. He asked me the name of my prosecutor. I replied, "Prosecutor James T. Borchard." He said it was the same one he had.

My attorney told me I was in the wrong courtroom, that I had to go across the hall to Judge Terry Clark's courtroom. As my mother and I got ready to leave, I glanced at Judge Thompson Jr. He was looking at me with pure hatred. I nudged my mother and asked her to look at him. She said, "I told you he wasn't any good."

As we entered Judge Terry Clark's courtroom, my mother looked for a seat to sit down. She sat next to Jose Douglas, who looked at her, smiled, and said hello. She looked over at him and said, "**NO! NO!** You're the officer that's trying to ruin my daughter's life!!!!" She ran up where my lawyer and I were seated. I started laughing at her, but she replied, "That's not funny. He knows I'm your mother!"

I noticed a tall, slender, handsome African-American man in a gray pin-striped suit with gold glasses, a short haircut, and a caramel complexion looking as fine as a glass of wine. He is what women call eye candy—good to look at. I could visualize him on the cover of the *Ebony* and *Jet* magazine. He looked so fine just standing in the front of the courtroom.

I glanced to the right of the courtroom at the judge. He seemed to be a small man with a light brown complexion. He wore glasses and seemed to have a very pleasant demeanor, nothing like the demeanor of Judge M. T. Thompson Jr. Then the handsome man began to speak. I realized he's the prosecutor. He looked at my attorney and asked, "What is it you have in your hand?"

My attorney handed him the paper. He read the paperwork from Superior Pontiac stating that nothing was wrong with the light over my license plate. He looked at the judge telling him to dismiss the charges since it's fixed. Now I looked at my attorney and said, "Pretty Boy lied. I didn't have anything 'fixed.' It was never broken."

"Yes, I know, but we have to get out of here." He started walking quickly. I followed him to a room at the opposite end of the hallway. He began talking to a female behind her desk telling her the charges were dropped, but then she handed him some type of paperwork which he signed. Then we moved quickly to Judge Thompson Jr.'s courtroom.

Police, Lawyers & Judges

As soon as we entered courtroom, the judge was calling my name. We approached the bench. This man was looking at me with pure hatred in his eyes. He spoke to me with venom rolling off his tongue. I thought to myself, this man acts as though I killed his whole family—his father, mother, sisters, brothers, wife, children, *and* the dog. As I listened he was trying to force me to pay bail again, and my attorney was telling him, "No! She's already paid bail for these charges. It's not fair to put another bail on her."

Judge Thompson stated, "I have concerns about her. She lives in Genesee County (30 miles south of Saginaw)."

"Your Honor," my attorney said, "my client has been here every time. She's always here on time. She works here in Saginaw."

Judge Thompson looked at me, shouting, "Count One is fleeing and eluding a police officer, which carries a maximum penalty of 5 years and up to $5,000 in fines. **YOU HIT A POLICE OFFICER!!!!!** Count Two is resisting, obstructing, and assaulting a police officer. It carries up to 2 years in prison and up to $2,000 in fines."

I stood there mute. My attorney and Judge Thompson Jr. went back and forth concerning my bail. Finally, the judge decided not to put any bail on me. He asked me if I was going to show up. I nodded my head yes. He told me if I didn't show up he was going to put a bench warrant out for my arrest and throw me back in jail, and I better not be a minute or even a second late or he would throw me in jail for that!!!!

My attorney said, "You don't have to speak to her in that manner. She will be here."

Once we were outside, I asked my attorney how I was going to get a fair hearing in that man's courtroom. He replied, "That's what I'm here for."

"Yes," I said, "but look at what happened today. They scheduled me to be in two courtrooms at once. If Judge Terry Clark hadn't been fair, there's no way I could have made it to Judge Thompson Jr.'s courtroom on time. That's why he was rude to me. I believe he wanted me to be late so I would go back to jail. That man is crazy!!!"

My attorney told me that his father was a minister and he was really not a bad guy. I replied, "His father was a minister; he's not. If he had any Christianity in him he wouldn't be trying to hang me by the words of a crooked prosecutor."

We said our good-byes. Before leaving, my attorney said, "I'm getting them on the November 15th. WATCH ME!!!"

As my mother and I walked to my vehicle she said, "I have never wanted to fight anyone as badly as I wanted to fight Judge Thompson Jr."

I said, "Mom, he's not worth it. *The Wizard of Oz* was written for him. He doesn't have a brain, heart, or courage, so don't waste your time. He's an idiot and a disgrace to his race; he's what the young people call a sell-out. The man is coming after me for no reason, other than the prosecutor told him to. They're mad at me for showing up with a lawyer and fighting back." The late Pastor Emeritus Brady instilled in me to always fight for justice. Bob Marley (1973) had a song titled "Get Up, Stand Up" which is about standing up for your rights and don't give up the fight. That's what I'm doing. When GOD gets ready, he will remove Judge Thompson and Prosecutor Borchard out of my way. GOD will make your enemies your footstool, and I'm going to rest my feet on their heads when it's over.

November 15, 2006, 4:00 P.M. was the date and time I had to be in Judge M. T. Thompson Jr.'s courtroom #306. I prayed and meditated and worked out physically. I ran and lifted weights to prepare myself. I read 1 Peter 4:12, "Beloved, think it not strange concerning the fiery trial which is to try you, as though some strange thing happened unto you." Jose Douglas will be on the witness stand lying. I feel sorry for him. It's obvious he never read Proverb 12:22, "Lying lips [are] abomination to the LORD: but they that deal truly [are] his delight."

Philippians 4:8 says, "Finally, brethren, whatsoever things are true, whatsoever things are honest, whatsoever things are just, whatsoever things are pure, whatsoever things are lovely, whatsoever things are of good report; if there be any virtue, and if there be any praise, think on these things." Other encouraging scriptures are: Philippians 4:13, "I can do all things through Christ which strengthens me," and Hebrews 13:6, "So that we may boldly say, The Lord is my helper, and I will not fear what man shall do unto me." I know Judge Thompson has something in store for me, and it won't be good!!!

November 15, 2006. My court date arrived. My mother and I drove to Saginaw, Michigan. As we entered the judge's courtroom, he seemed to be in a good mood. He was alert while listening to all the evidence concerning the case before mine. However, that attentiveness seemed to fade away when it was my turn.

STATE OF MICHIGAN
IN THE 70th JUDICIAL DISTRICT COURT FOR SAGINAW COUNTY
THE PEOPLE OF THE STATE OF MICHIGAN
Case No. 06-9394-FY vs. Kim Davis, Defendant.
Preliminary Examination
BEFORE THE HONORABLE M. T. THOMPSON, JR., DISTRICT JUDGE
Saginaw, Michigan, Wednesday, November 15, 2006
Appearances:
For the People:

RANDY L. PRICE P53404
Saginaw County Prosecutor's Office
111 S. Michigan Avenue
Saginaw, Michigan 48602
(989) 790-5330

TABLE OF CONTENTS
WITNESSES: PEOPLE
Jose Douglas
Direct Examination by Mr. Price
Cross-Examination by: Mr. Frank
Redirect Examination by: Mr. Price
No Recross-Examination
Kevin Jay Kratz
Direct Examination by Mr. Price
Cross-Examination by Mr. Frank
Saginaw, Michigan
Wednesday, November 15, 2006, at about 4:01 P.M.
The Court: Judge Thompson, Jr.
Prosecuting Attorney: Mr. Price
Defense Attorney Mr. Frank and Defendant Ms. Davis present
THE COURT: The Court will take up the matter of People vs. Kim Davis

MR. PRICE: May it please the Court, Randy Price on behalf of the people. At this time, the People are ready to proceed.

THE COURT: You may proceed.

MR. PRICE: Your Honor, I call Jose Douglas.

THE COURT: I'm sorry I can't hear you.

MR. PRICE: Your Honor, I call Jose Douglas.

MR. FRANK: Is he going to be your only witness?

MR. PRICE: Yes.

THE BAILIFF: Raise your right hand for me, please.

You solemnly swear the testimony you are about to give in the cause now pending shall be the truth, the whole truth, nothing but the truth so help you God?

OFFICER DOUGLAS: Yes.

THE BAILIFF: Be seated, watch your step.

JOSE DOUGLAS called as a witness at about 4:02 P.M., testified as follows:

DIRECT EXAMINATION

Sir, can you state your name for the record, please?

Jose Douglas.

Where do you work?

I work for the Buena Vista Police Department.

And what do you do there?

I'm a police officer at the Buena Vista Police Department.

And, sir, I want to, ah, draw your attention to September 28th of this year. Were you working for Buena Vista Police Department?

Yes sir.

Do you recall what shift you were working that day?

Yes sir, I was working the midnight shift.

And what hours does that encompass?

That's 9 P.M. to 7 A.M.

And around 11:30, twelve midnight on that date, ah, were you in the area of Outer Drive and Lapeer Street, which is in Buena Vista Township, the County of Saginaw, State of Michigan?

Yes sir.

And you were in a fully marked patrol vehicle?

Yes sir.

And by meaning fully marked patrol vehicle, this had the lights on the outside?
Yes sir.
And were you also fully uniformed or in a police officer uniform?
Yes sir.
And at that location did you see a vehicle that drew your attention?
Yes sir.
What kind, type of vehicle was it, if you can recall?
It was an urn, white, ah, Grand Prix.
And what was the reason that this vehicle drew your attention to it?
Because the registration light was out.
Did you try to pull this vehicle over?
Yes sir.
And try to pull this vehicle over, how did you do that? Did you turn on the lights?
Yes sir.
The overhead lights?
Yes sir.
Did the vehicle stop?
No sir.
What did it do?
It slowed down like it was going to stop. And then it kept on going. It never came to a complete stop.
And did it accelerate rapidly?
MR. FRANK: I am going to object.
THE WITNESS: No.
MR. FRANK: Leading question.
MR. PRICE: I'll cha—I'll rephrase. Once it looked like it was going to stop, it did not stop?
MR. FRANK: The question's been asked and answered.
MR. PRICE: I'll move on. What did it do after it didn't stop?
It continued on.
And how far did it continue on?
It continued on, ah, about a mile.
THE COURT: Did you have your lights and sirens on?

THE WITNESS: Yes sir. I activated my lights, and then I turned my sirens on after she didn't stop.

THE COURT: And the car continued for a mile after you activated them?

THE WITNESS: Yes sir.

THE COURT: And how close were you to the vehicle?

THE WITNESS: Sir, I do not know exactly how close I was. I don't know the distance; I was ah-

THE COURT: Well, were you two, three, four, five, ten car lengths, five blocks back?

THE WITNESS: Urn, I would say maybe a car length.

MR. PRICE: How fast were you going?

I didn't look at my speedometer. But, ah, it was about maybe 30 miles an hour.

What's the, ah, the speed limit in that area?

The speed limit in that area is, ah, I think is 45.

And, ah, this . . . this vehicle continued for a mile?

Yes sir.

Did it eventually stop?

Yes sir.

Where did it stop?

It stopped . . .

Do you recall?

On Outer near . . . Can I look at my report to refresh my memory?

If it will refresh your memory.

Outer and Norman.

And when it stopped, did you approach the vehicle?

Yes sir.

Did you make contact with the driver?

Yes sir.

Was the driver outside the car or inside the car when you made contact?

She was inside the vehicle.

And that driver, do you see that person in the courtroom today?

Yes sir.

Can you point to that person and describe what they are wearing, please?

She's right over there wearing the orange shirt.

MR. PRICE: Your Honor, may the record reflect identification of the Defendant.

THE COURT: It does.

MR. PRICE: When you made contact with her, can you describe her demeanor?

Yes, when I got out of the vehicle and approached her vehicle, ah, you know, I ordered her to get out, and, ah, she was in the vehicle still just looking straight-ahead.

THE COURT: Was she alone in the vehicle?

THE WITNESS: Yes sir.

Did it appear as if she knew or did she acknowledge to you that she knew that you were there?

She didn't do anything at the time, at first contact.

So what did you do when she did not get out of the vehicle for the first command?

I, ah, ah, I opened the door. Opened the door and ordered her out of the vehicle, and then she got out of the vehicle.

And when she got out of the vehicle, what did you have her do?

I had her stand to the side of the vehicle.

Did she? You commanded her to do that?

Well, yes.

And did she follow the command?

That's my first command. No sir, ah, when she stepped out, when she first stepped out of the vehicle she, she got out. And she was waving her hands and stuff, and, and ah, you know, at first I was just trying to calm her down, and then I ordered her to step to the side of the vehicle.

And once you had her step to the side of the vehicle, she did that, in fact?

Yes.

Did you have her do anything when she stepped to the side of the vehicle?

No sir, urn, she kept ah, she was, she kept talking to me, and she ah, well, she wasn't talking to me. She wanted to know why we pulled her over. She was swearing. Um . . . And then that's when I ordered her to the back of the vehicle.

And she went to the back of the vehicle?

She went to the back of the vehicle.

And when she got to the back of the vehicle, what did, what then did you do?

I ordered her to put her hands to the back on the trunk of her vehicle.

And what was the reason that you wanted her to put her hands on the trunk?

Because I, ah, you know, I was trying to control her. Like I said, she was swearing and everything.

Did she put her hands on the vehicle?

She put her hands on the vehicle.

Then what did you do?

Then she took her hand off of the vehicle.

And what did you do?

And then I ordered her to put her hands back on the vehicle.

And did she do that?

No, that's when she took both hands off the vehicle and turned around.

And at this time, were you trying to search her, search her person?

No, no sir.

And did you tell her to place her hands back on the car?

Yes.

Did she do that?

No.

So what did you have to do?

Well, after I told her to place her hands back on the vehicle, you know, she didn't put her hands on the vehicle. And, ah, I tried to, she was swearing and moving around, and I tried to grab her to physically put her back on the, put her hands back on the vehicle. When I tried to do that she pulled away, and then that's when, ah, me and Officer Patterson handcuffed her.

Did she ever threaten you at, at any point in this con—, this, ah, incident?

You said threaten?

Yes.

Yes, she threatened, um . . .

What did she say?

She said, "I'll whip your ass."

Eventually you did get her handcuffed, is that correct then?

Yes sir.

And again the reason for pulling her over was why?

I pulled her over because she, ah, went to the east side, she was traveling northbound. I noticed her registration light was out, and then she swerved over, crossing the fog line on the east side of the roadway. When she was, ah, behind the, or in the rear, let me back up.

When you had her go back to the rear of the vehicle, ah, and place her hands on the car, did she ever try to reach for any of her pockets?

Yeah, looked like she was reaching toward her pocket.

Did you ask her to stop that?

No, that's what ah, she, when I told her to put her hands on the vehicle, I didn't tell her to stop reaching, I just told her to put her hands back on the vehicle.

You stated that she was yelling things. Was she yelling obscenities?

MR. FRANK: Your Honor, that question has been asked and answered.

MR. PRICE: I don't think it has, Your Honor.

MR. FRANK: Leading.

THE COURT: Overruled. You may answer the question.

THE WITNESS: Yes, she was.

MR. PRICE: Thank you, sir. I have nothing further, Your Honor.

CROSS-EXAMINATION

MR. FRANK: You indicated that her tire went on the fog line of travel?

Yes sir.

Correct?

Yes.

And was that when you were one car length behind her?

Yes sir.

And that's when, ah, in relation to those streets that you list in your report, do you know what street you were by when that happened?

That was near, that's when we crossed right over the 675 overpass.

Urn, urn, this was a white 2005 Pontiac four-door Grand Prix?

Yes sir.

And, urn, you say in your report the venue was, ah, at Holland near 675?

Not Holland.

Well, you got your report there?

Yes sir, I have my report.

On page, ah, 2 of 3 where it says venue?

Yes sir.

You say venue Saginaw County Buena Vista Township, Holland Avenue, I 675.

Yes sir, that's what—

Is that correct?

—on the report, but it happened on Outer Drive.

Well, I understand that. So my question to you is, did you, were you at that Motel 8 on the corner of Holland and Outer Drive when you first saw this vehicle?

No sir.

Were you at the Outer, were you at Holland and Outer Drive prior to traveling northbound on Outer Drive?

Well, I understand that.

So my question to you is, did you, were you at that Motel 8 on the corner of Holland and Outer Drive when you first saw this vehicle?

Yes sir, that's what—

—Is that correct?

on the report, but it happened on Outer Drive.

Well, I understand that. So my question to you is, did you, were you at that Motel 8 on the corner of Holland and Outer Drive when you first saw this vehicle?

No sir.

Were you at the Outer, were you at Holland and Outer Drive prior to traveling northbound on Outer Drive?

We was at—

Do you know where you were at?

I was at Outer and near Perkins.

You were where?

Outer and Perkins.

Were you just driving down the road?

I believe at first I was on the side of the roadway, and then that's when I saw her.

On the side of the roadway, is that what you are telling us now?

Yes sir.

At, where at?

I wasn't at Holland.

It was at, let me see, Holland, no, not Holland, Outer near Perkins. Perkins and Outer. So you were not at the 8 Motel near Holland and Outer Drive prior to, ah, seeing this car?

NO.

All right.

Now, you indicate, ah, that, well, where is Perkins in relation to, ah, the street known by the name of, ah, Lapeer. Is that Lapeer? Where's Perkins in relation to Lapeer?

Lapeer. Yeah, that's south of Lapeer.

Perkins, let me see. Lapeer is, Lapeer is north of Perkins. And so in relation to you, you were in what direction, you say, when you were at near Perkins?

I'm sorry, I was, ah, I was in . . .

Where were you in position?

I was at Lapeer. I made a mistake.

Pardon me?

I made a mistake. I was, it was Lapeer and Outer, not Perkins and Outer, and it was a mistake.

So now you are at Lapeer stationary?

That's where I was, I was on Lapeer and, ah, near Outer. That's when, that's when I noticed it.

So what you are telling us now is that you were on Lapeer near . . .

No, I was on Outer Drive.

Well, you just told us you were on Lapeer near Outer. That's your testimony; now you're on Outer Drive, is that not true?

I was on Outer. The vehicle was traveling on Outer, and I was traveling on Outer.

And where were you coming from?

I was coming from . . . I just did another traffic stop and I was on my way to Flying Jays.

You were where, going where?

I was on my way to Flying Jays.

I see. You were on your way to Flying Jays for what reason?

I was, I was going to take my ninety-four, that's lunch.

Oh. So you were on your way to Flying Jays for lunch?

Yes.

Did you ask her if she was high, was high or on drugs?

Yes sir.

Now Lapeer dead ends into Outer Drive, does it not?

Yes sir, Lapeer does dead end.

And then, ah, at that point in time, we have, ah, ah, any incline up over ah, East West Road, do we not?

East West Road?

Yeah.

Outer Drive goes over on East West Road like an overpass type of deal?

Yes, it's 675.

All right, that's the East and West Road?

Yes sir.

And from Lapeer, the next road directly north of that is, ah, would be Wadsworth, right?

Yes sir.

And the distance between Lapeer and Wadsworth is four-tenths of a mile, approximately, isn't that correct?

I don't know. I've never measured it. I didn't know.

Yeah, well, maybe you should. And then, ah, the distance between, ah, you said this car stopped at Fuller, near Fuller?

No, I didn't say that. The car stopped, looked at me. It stopped at Norman.

Pardon me?

It stopped at Norman.

It stopped at Norman?

(no verbal answer)

All right. And so, from Wadsworth, you have that Irving, is the next one north?

Uh-huh.

Monmouth, correct?

Yes.

Exeter?

Yes sir.

Sears?

Yes sir.

And you have the railroad tracks where North Street and ah, and you have the railroad tracks where North Street and ah, and ah, Norman Avenue, is that correct?

Yes sir.

And the distance, ah, between Wadsworth and, ah, Norman is approximately four-tenths of a mile, is it not?

Like I said, I don't know.

All right.

Now, where in relation to the Lapeer point of reference and Norman point of reference did you put on your overhead lights?

I put my overheads on just before we got to Wadsworth. Between Lapeer and Wadsworth, that's when I activated my lights.

All right. And so if you were stationary, ah, and this vehicle was traveling at 30 miles an hour and you got four-tenths of a mile, ah, between Lapeer and Wadsworth, wouldn't this vehicle have passed Wadsworth already?

I don't know.

All right.

Now, you say you activated a siren someplace along this spectrum of roads. After Wadsworth and before Norman, where in this, where in this scale of things did you do that?

I activated my lights?

No, sirens.

Sirens?

Yeah.

I activated my sirens when I saw that she wasn't, when she—

Where was that? I just want to know where it was.

That was just—

You don't know what's in her mind.

That was just, ah, I say north of Wadsworth.

How far north of Wadsworth?

Like I, I don't know.

Was it, ah, by Irving? Or was it past Monmouth or Exeter or Sears?

No, just—

You remember?

It's just before I got to the next street which was, the next street passed, ah, the next street passed Wadsworth.

Are you sure about that?

Yes, I activated my sirens.

All right. Now, on the east side of the road traveling north Outer Drive you have guardrails, don't you?

Yes.

They are guardrails that go from Wadsworth all the way to Norman?

Yes.

Correct?

(no verbal answer)

And, ah, to the east of those guardrails is this huge deep ditch.

Yes.

Correct?

Correct.

And ah, these guardrails are for the purpose of keeping motorists safe from going into that big huge ditch, right?

Yes sir.

Now, there's a fog line on that paved portion of the roadway. Do you know that to be a fact?

Yes sir.

But there is not enough room for a vehicle to pull off of the traveled portion of that roadway between the rail and the fog line, isn't that true?

That's true but that's not where she went off the roadway at.

She also told you after you pulled her over that she didn't feel safe in pulling over by all those guardrails and the lights that she felt weren't enough for her safety. She told you that, didn't she?

She told me that she didn't pull over because the road was too dark.

No, she, well, you even write in your—

She didn't mention—

—report, sir.

She didn't mention anything about the guardrails.

She said that she didn't feel safe and that she wasn't going to pull over on a dark road. In her mind, it was a dark road. To you, she said that, did she not?

Yes, she said that.

All right.

There was no collision or accident involved in this matter?

No sir.

She doesn't have a prior conviction for fourth-degree fleeing and eluding, does she?

I'm going to object to that; that's irrelevant in this matter, Your Honor.

THE COURT: It is.

MR. FRANK: Oh, I don't think so, Judge.

THE COURT: And why don't you?

MR. FRANK: Because the statute that specifically addresses it is 257.602a (3).

THE COURT: How does the statute address it?

MR. FRANK: Want me to show it to you?

THE COURT: Yeah, you can tell us what the statute says. Mr. Price questions your interpretation.

MR. FRANK: Well, it says—Well . . .

THE COURT: read it.

MR. FRANK: "Except as provided in subsection (4) and (5), an individual who violates ... section (1)—" which is the driving of a motor vehicle who does not head, daa, daa, daa, who violates that section (1) is guilty of a third-degree fleeing and eluding ah, "... if 1 or more of the following circumstances apply." Part C is, "The individual has a prior conviction of fourth-degree fleeing and eluding."

THE COURT: Okay.

MR. FRANK: So it is relevant.

THE COURT: You can answer the question.

THE WITNESS: Can you repeat the question again?

MR. FRANK: My question was, this person here does not have a conviction for fourth-degree fleeing, fleeing and eluding, does she? Does she?

Not to my knowledge.

She also told you that, ah, she thought you were after somebody else and not her, didn't she?

Ah, I don't recall that.

Right. Now listen, you were driving a marked vehicle, you say?

Yes sir.

Do you have some way to identify that vehicle you were using that night?

No sir.

Is there a number on it, like number two car, number five car or something?

I don't remember exactly which car I was driving that night.

Do you get assigned different cars?

We just pick whichever car we want and take it.

You have some, some way of noting what car you have for a particular night?

No sir, we just—

You don't have to register it?

No sir.

When you come on duty you don't have to say, I got car number two?

No sir, we just jump in the vehicle and go.

And so you don't know what vehicle it was?

No sir, I do not recall.

All right.

Dispatch might have, ah, proof of which vehicle I was in.

Now when you were transporting, ah, Miss Davis here, you, you had radio traffic; you made radio communication, did you not?

Yes sir.

And you called in for mileage verification of some sort, do you remember that?

Yes sir.

Who did you call?

I called dispatch.

Central Dispatch?

Yes sir.

Okay. And when you were in this conversation, ah, you also asked them what you ought to charge her with, didn't you?

No.

And that there was some response in terms of codes that you received back? Do you remember that?

Ah, no, when you call, when we take a female subject in, we have to call out the mileage, that was it. That's the only radio traffic.

Did she also inform you that she was on her way to work, and did she tell you where she worked?

I can't recall where she worked.

She was on her way to Delphi?

I can't recall.

And she wanted to call her boss and say, ah, that, ah, she wouldn't be reporting in because of your activity, is that correct?

Yeah, she did say that.

Yes.

MR. PRICE: Object. This is irrelevant. It is.

THE COURT: Sustained.

All right.

MR. FRANK: Not all of those streets are lighted, are they? Those cross streets to Outer Drive?

All the lights were working that night.

That wasn't my question, sir. My question to you is, that not all the cross streets with Outer Drive between the Lapeer and Norman Avenue aren't all lighted, are they?

I don't know whether they were lighted down the streets or not, but on Outer Drive where we were traveling they were all lit.

My question to you then is, ah, are you saying that every intersection had a light?

I don't know whether every intersection has a light, but I know that all the lights that were on that street were working that night.

What other, whatever lights were out there, you believe they were working?

I know they were working.

You did tell her that you were going to search her car for drugs?

I told her that we were gonna search her car.

My question, sir, was, did you tell her you were gonna search her car for drugs?

No sir.

And you found some clear plastic jugs in the trunk, did you not?

Yes sir.

And did you tell her at that time, we got her, or we got her with moonshine?

No sir.

MR. PRICE: Your Honor, it's getting a little too out of hand, Your Honor. I would object to the relevancy.

THE COURT: Sustained.

MR. FRANK: So you and, ah, the, who was the other officer that was there?

Officer Patterson.

Anybody else?

Other officers showed up later.

Who?

Officer Villanueva and Sergeant Baker.

Was this after you had secured her in handcuffs?

Yes sir.

Officer Patterson was there; as a matter of fact, he was involved in the chase also. He was there when I first got her out.

Let me ask you this, did you treat this woman with respect that night?

Yes sir, I did.

You didn't use any derogatory remarks to her during this investigation before you secured her in handcuffs?

No more than yelling, ordering her to get out of the vehicle, not that I can recall.

Now with regards to her getting out of the car, ah, where did she go when she got out of the car?

She stepped just to the side of the vehicle.

And how long were you there?

Ah, I wasn't timing it. Just maybe a minute or so.

And then where did you go from that position?

To the back of her vehicle.

At that time had you placed her under arrest?

Well, she was under arrest for, for fleeing and eluding.

Listen, sir. At the time that you had her at the back of the vehicle, did you place her under arrest at that particular point in time?

Not at that particular point in time.

Did you at any time tell her why you wanted her to get out of the car and go back to the back of the vehicle?

Ah, no, I just ordered her to get out of the vehicle.

At any time before you put the handcuffs on her, did you ever tell her why she was being ordered out of her car?

No, I didn't tell her.

So initially, you signed a complaint against her for fleeing and eluding fourth-degree; is that correct?

MR. PRICE: Your Honor, I am going to object. I don't think it's relevant.

THE COURT: Sustained.

MR. PRICE: Thank you.

MR. FRANK: Juncture. Nothing further, Judge, at this time.

REDIRECT EXAMINATION

MR. PRICE: Officer, are you certain of the speed limit in that area?

MR. FRANK: Your Honor, that question has been asked and answered; he just testified to it.

THE COURT: It has been.

MR. PRICE: This witness, Your Honor.

THE COURT: I don't have any other questions.

I've got a few, but I am not going to let them trigger any additional questions from either side.

Now, as you're traveling north on Outer Drive, all the streets run dead end into Outer Drive, don't they?

THE WITNESS: Yes, from ah, no. Wadsworth doesn't.

THE COURT: Well, with the exception of Wadsworth. If you go from Janes north all the way to Lapeer, don't all the other streets run dead end into Wadsworth, I mean into Outer?

THE WITNESS: Janes and Lapeer are the only streets there.

THE COURT: No, if you go from Janes all the way, all the others run dead into Outer Drive?

THE WITNESS: Yes sir. Well, Lapeer is a dead end.

THE COURT: And, well, I said to Lapeer.

THE WITNESS: Okay.

THE COURT: And contrary to what Attorney Frank said, there is not a guardrail all the way down there. In some cases, there's just the big ditch, isn't there?

THE WITNESS: No, there's not a guardrail all the way down. Urn, well, between the point where she was, ah, there was a guardrail. But just as you cross over the hill there's, a, where she went over to the side of the roadway there, ah, there wasn't one in that area.

THE COURT: All right. Where exactly did you activate your lights?

I activated my lights, um, between, between Lapeer and Wadsworth.

THE COURT: Okay. And how far did she continue after you activated your lights and siren?

THE WITNESS: She continued on all the way up to, ah, just Norman, just, well, excuse me.

THE COURT: How far is that?

THE WITNESS: That's, ah, like I said, I don't know the distance exactly. But, ah, you know, it's about a mile.

MR. FRANK: Your Honor, for the record, I can tell you that I checked that distance, and it's like approximately four-tenths of a mile, if that's what Your Honor wants to know.

THE COURT: Well, during this period, you said that she didn't go beyond 30 miles per hour?

THE WITNESS: No, not, ah, I mean, I didn't look at my, ah, well, I wasn't looking at my speedometer. You know, I was busing, talking on the radio. But she was going about 30 miles an hour. Judging from how fast we were going.

THE COURT: All right, you may, you may step down.

(At about 4:42 P.M. witness excused)

MR. PRICE: Your Honor, I wish to call Kevin Kratz, just to establish the speed limit in that area.

THE BAILIFF: You solemnly swear the testimony you are about to give in the cause now pending shall be the truth, the whole truth, nothing but the truth, so help you?

DETECTIVE KRATZ: I do.

KEVIN JAY KRATZ called as a witness at about 4:43 P.M., testified as follows.

DIRECT EXAMINATION BY MR. PRICE.

Sir, can you state your name for the record, please?

Kevin Jay Kratz.

Where, K-R-A-T-Z, do you work, sir?

Buena Vista Police Department.

And what do you do there?

I'm a detective.

How long have you been working for the Buena Vista Police Department?

Nine years in June.

And you were a road patrol officer before you became detective?

I was.

And, ah, are you familiar with the area of South Outer Drive, Lapeer, ah, Monmouth, Exeter, or Sears, that area?

I am.

What is the speed limit in that area?

Thirty-five miles an hour.

And that's in the Buena Vista Township, ah, County of Saginaw, State of Michigan?

It is.

Thank you, sir

Mr. PRICE: I have nothing further, Your Honor.

THE COURT: Absent any cross you may step down. Is there any cross?

CROSS-EXAMINATION

MR. FRANK: Oh, ah, between Wadsworth and Norman, ah, are there any posted signs there on the east side of the road?

I don't recall off the top of my head if there are or not.

MR. FRANK: I have no further questions.

THE COURT: You may step down.

THE WITNESS: Thank you.

(At about 4:44 P.M. witness excused)

MR. PRICE: I don't have any other witnesses for this examination, Your Honor.

THE COURT: Defense has any witnesses?

MR. FRANK: Ah, none.

THE COURT: All right.

The Court has listened carefully to the testimony of Officer Douglas which was confusing and inconsistent, to say the least. Ah, I would expect a patrol officer to know the area. And the streets changed, where she was stopped changed, where he was coming from changed.

The testimony was just confusing and inconsistent.

And despite that the testimony as to what occurred after she was stopped and her resisting and failing to follow instructions does come across clear. Ah, I am not prepared to base findings with respect to Count One on the testimony I've heard. And so I am not going to bind her over on the fleeing and eluding just because of the confusing and inconsistent nature of the testimony that I've heard. Among other things, I would expect officers to read their reports before they come to court. And get the street names and their locations straight in their minds before they take the stand. But I am not prepared to bind her over on the testimony I heard with respect to Count One. I am going to bind her over to stand trial in circuit court on Count Two.

MR. PRICE: Thank you, Your Honor.

MR. FRANK: Thank you for your time, Judge.

(At about 4:45 P.M. proceeding concluded)

Police, Lawyers & Judges

STATE OF MICHIGAN, COUNTY OF SAGINAW

I, M. Kelli Scorsone, certify that this transcript, consisting of 36 pages, is a complete, true, and correct transcript, of the proceedings and testimony taken in this case on Wednesday, November 15, 2006.

My lawyer has to go to the judge's chambers. He asked me to wait at the table for him. My mother came to me, ready to go into Judge Thompson's chambers to jump on him. She has her purse ready to use as a weapon. She asked me, **"HOW CAN YOU SIT HERE SO CALM AND COOL?"**

I replied, "I'll share with you later." She kept talking about the judge. I said, "Mom, calm down. His court reporter is sitting there, and she can hear you."

The court reporter replied, "I won't tell him what you're saying."

My mother answered, "You can tell him if you want to. I'm the Momma Bear protecting my cub. If he comes back out here, I will tell him what I said. **HE'S NO GOOD!!! HE'S LOW-DOWN!!!!** He had it in for my daughter, and he doesn't know her. What the judge says doesn't matter. She was on her way to work, but if she was coming out of a crack house or leaving a liquor store with a bunch of liquor in her car, it would have been allowed in court, so don't tell me he's not a rotten judge!!! He couldn't look at her when he ruled against her. Also, he was falling asleep, with his head rocking back and forth as though he was in a rocking chair."

"Mom," I said, "did you see the way he looked at me when Douglas told that lie that I said I was going to whip his ass when I saw him out somewhere? Who in their right mind would threaten a police officer that's carrying a Taser, gun, and a nightstick? That man is sick. He doesn't deserve to be a judge. He knows I don't know my way around in the Saginaw area. I just work here. Voters should come and observe people that they put in office. Just because this man is supposed to be a Christian people voted for him. He does not deserve to sit on a bench. He doesn't have compassion or understanding. He's not biased; he's pro police, and he leans toward the prosecutor. He never once said one word to Prosecutor Borchard."

At that moment, my attorney came from the chambers. I was relieved to see him, because I didn't know how long I could contain my mother. My attorney and I began to walk out of the courtroom.

I noticed my mother wasn't with me. I turned around to find her staring at the door to Judge M. T. Thompson Jr.'s chambers. I grabbed her by her arm, politely telling her, "Mom, you cannot hit a judge. They will put you away for a long time." She finally calmed down. As we walked, I was holding her hand to keep her from going back to the courtroom.

My attorney looked at me and said, "You did nothing at all. You were up front with me about everything."

After that, an African-American female appeared in the hallway that had been working in Judge Thompson's courtroom. She patted my attorney on the back and told him he did a good job. She knew Buena Vista like the back of her hand. I looked at her, and she smiled at me. I felt she knew I was innocent. She told me good luck.

Once we got outside, Jose Douglas was standing there waiting for a ride. Mom wanted a piece of him. I pulled her toward my vehicle and told her, "I'm taking you out to dinner, to TGI Friday's in Saginaw Township." Once we sat down to order our food she asked me, "Why are you so calm?"

I explained to her I was chosen for this mission and please not interrupt me before I finished. "Mom, I'm a runner. We have laid-back demeanors. I never would have hollered back at Officer Timothy W. Patterson. I usually would have ignored him. That's why I believe I was chosen for this assignment."

My birthday is February 11th. That's the day that Nelson Mandela was released from prison in 1990. Rosa Parks's birthday is February 4th. Frederick Douglass's birthday is February 14th or 18th. On February 12, 1909, the NAACP was established. Dr. Carter G. Woodson established Black History Month, and Woodson is my grandmother's maiden name. The month he chose was February. I'm a UAW member. The sit-down strike of 1937 began December 30, 1936, and ended February 11, 1937. Walter Reuther (president, UAW) strongly supported the Civil Rights movement; Reuther was an active supporter of African-American civil rights and participated in both the March on Washington for Freedom and Jobs (August 1963) and the Selma to Montgomery March (March 1965). He stood beside Martin Luther King Jr. while he made the "I Have a Dream" speech during the 1963 March on Washington. After King's assassination in Memphis, Tennessee, the UAW made a donation of $50,000 for the striking sanitation workers. I believe GOD had prepared me for this fight.

SEPTEMBER 11, 1977

Grace Emmanuel Baptist Church

1513 KENT   FLINT, MICHIGAN 48503

"Every Member Loyalty Day"

Dr. Martin Luther King, Sr.
Pastor Emeritus of the Ebenezer Baptist Church
Atlanta, Georgia

"A Giant Of A Man"

Rev. Lindell L. Brady, Pastor

"The Church Where God's Program Comes First"

Weekly Opportunities

Grace Unity Bible Class — Wednesday 10:00 A.M.
Mrs. Jessie Brady, Teacher
916 Lippincott Blvd.

Wednesday Night Prayer Service
7:00 P.M.
Leader for this week, Rev. Wilbert Campbell

Youth Fellowship
Friday
Juniors and Teens — 6:00-7:00 P.M.

Sunday School
9:30 A.M.
Deacon Larry Kemp, Superintendent
Classes for all ages

Our Sick And Shut In

Mr. Crawford Pendergross .... Room 611, Hurley
Mr. Raymond Vaughn .... 1967 Crocker Ave.
Mr. George Stith .... 3705 Evergreen Parkway

Thought For The Day

Who will miss you most this once at church? **God will.**

Tithes and Offerings for Last Sunday — $3,633

EVERY MEMBER LOYALTY DAY

ORDER OF WORSHIP

Morning Service, 11:00 A.M.

Prelude and Quiet Meditation
Call to Worship
Processional Hymn No. 7 .... (Stanzas 1,2,4)
Prayer in Unison:
    Our Father and our God, we thank Thee for this Thy Church and for the in-gathering of our Church Family to rededicate ourselves anew, to total Christian Commitment. We praise Thee in this sacred hour of worship and ask that Thou wilt give us spiritual strength, guidance, and a new sense of direction. Bless our service today and help us to be better Christians, as a result of it. We pray in the Name of the One who loved the Church, and gave Himself for It, even Christ Jesus our Lord. Amen.

Congregational Hymn No. 92 .... Stanzas 1, 2, 4
Responsive Reading .... Selection 443
Adult Choir Selection
Scripture Reading .... Phillipians 4:4-13
Moments of Meditation and Prayer .... No. 117
Welcome to Visitors
Announcements
Dedication of Tithes and Offerings
Adult Choir Selection
Introduction of the Speaker .... Pastor Brady
Sermon .... Dr. Martin Luther King, Sr.
Invitation to Discipleship No. 406 .... Stanzas 1, 2, 4
Altar Call
Free Will Offering
Closing Hymn No. 137 .... Stanzas 1, 4
Benediction and Threefold Amen

Announcements

We are happy to have the eminent Dr. Martin Luther King, Sr. Pastor Emeritus of Ebenezer Baptist Church, Atlanta, Georgia as our Guest Speaker today. Welcome Dr. King.

Today is the Eleventh Annual Observance of "Every Member Loyalty Day." This special day is designated as the "Ingathering" of all the members of our Church Family. It is a day of spiritual renewal and rededication to God and His Church. We ask each member to re-evaluate his or her life as it relates to Christian duty and faithfulness, and to respond to each of these, as Christ would have us to do. **We will not have any evening service.**

All Ushers are asked to meet Saturday at 1:00 P.M. for a brief Bible Study and meeting with the Pastor, followed by drills with President Robert Richardson III. Be sure to attend this meeting.

Next Sunday at 4:00 P.M. we will fellowship with Mt. Sinai Missionary Baptist Church, 1215 E. Downey in observance of their Annual Choir Day. Our Pastor will bring the message, our Adult and Vesper Choirs will sing, and our Ushers will serve. Plan now to attend.

SEVEN MINDS

1. **Mind your tongue** — Do not let it speak hasty, cruel, unkind, or wicked words.
2. **Mind your eyes** — Do not permit them to look on sinful books, pictures, or objects.
3. **Mind your ears** — Do not suffer them to listen to wicked words, or idle gossip.
4. **Mind your lips** — Do not let profanity foul them, nor strong drink pass them.
5. **Mind your hands** — Do not let them steal, fight, or engage in any manner of evil.
6. **Mind your feet** — Do not let them walk in the steps of the wicked.
7. **Mind your heart** — Do not let the love of sin dwell in it. Do not give it to Satan, but ask Jesus to make it His Throne.

My cousin, the late Rev. Randy Richardson, always said, "Having the Father, Son, and Holy Ghost in your corner was like having the tenacity of Jack Johnson, the strength of Joe Louis, and the speed of Muhammad Ali." How can I lose? Plus, you have to remember, I shook the hand of the late Rev. Dr. Martin Luther King Sr.

My mom looked at me and told me she didn't believe in numerology, but she liked the case I laid out before her. She told me she has the bulletin from every Member Loyalty Day, and the date was September 11, 1977.

I was ready to jump up out of my seat. That was conformation for me to FIGHT! The *F* in February stands for **FIGHT BACK!!!**

November 20, 2006. I received a call from my aunt Lee Black. She's a retired police officer, and she was questioning me about my case. I was happy to hear from her. None of my other relatives had contacted me regarding anything about my case except my uncle Michael Black, who is a retired deputy sheriff. He never called me directly, but he always called my mother regarding my case. My aunt wanted to know if I thought they could see that I was a female. I replied, "No, it was dark." She then asked if I had filed a complaint with the Buena Vista Internal Affairs Department. I replied no. She explained to me that one of the arresting officers could have a record and it needed to be investigated. "Make sure you fight back to let them know you are somebody. Once the police get you in their system, they don't want to let you go."

November 21, 2006, 1:55 P.M. I entered the Buena Vista Police Department and met with Sgt. Vincent Breckenridge. He's African-American, around 40–50 years old, stands between 5 foot 11 and 6 foot. He's stocky and weighs around 240 pounds. He had a pleasant personality. He led me to a room where we sat down at exactly 2:01 P.M. I flipped my cell phone on to make sure of the time, then I introduced myself to him. Obviously, he heard of me. He was stunned that I was sitting across from him. I told him I was here to see if they had an Internal Affairs Department. He answered No, and then I asked why not? He replied, "We are a small department."

I told him I was there to file a complaint on the profanity that was written up by Jose Douglas and Jaime Villanueva. She had stated I called her a "stupid bitch." The only thing I said to her was keep her hands off me. I wanted to know why she slammed me into the cruiser and why Timothy W. Patterson was going around telling citizens of United States of American, land of the free, home of the brave, that they have "no rights in Buena Vista." "Is this the way you train your officers?"

He answered, "Everybody curses when they get pulled over. You are a liar."

I replied, "So what you are telling me is that you tell your officers to pad up a report to use that against a person's character. Let me tell you something, you bring those three lying police officers to court, and I will have 30 people there who have never heard me speak in that manner!!!"

He asked, "Didn't you have a lawyer?"

"Yes, I do!!" I replied.

"Well, we dropped the charges against you; go after the prosecutor."

"No, I'm going after you," I replied, then I asked, "Why don't you have cameras in the cruisers?"

At that moment the phone rang. It was the chief of police (Brian Booker). Some test was given to the officers. I heard him saying Timothy W. Patterson was the only one who passed. Once Sgt. Breckenridge returned, I asked him some history on Officer Patterson. He told me I should investigate Jose Douglas, that he was out of Detroit and he might have a record and to have my lawyer do a background check on him. I told him Timothy W. Patterson was the evil one. He said have your lawyer run Jose Douglas's record. At that moment I decided to leave. He handed me his business card and wrote his direct line on the back of the card.

On my drive home, I couldn't get over him turning on Jose Douglas. Timothy W. Patterson is the one with the record, I believed, and with time, I would find out. Timothy Patterson was pure evil. He had no business working with people. He needed to work in a cubicle by himself, with no contact with people at all.

November 27, 2006, 11:06 A.M. I was watching FOX News, Channel 2, out of Detroit, Michigan. They were reporting about a fake cop in the Auburn Hills area. The first thing they told women to do was go to a lighted area if they are being stopped. I started laughing. I wondered if I should call Buena Vista Police Department and inform Officer Timothy

W. Patterson what the news media just reported. No, I better leave that man alone. He might try to arrest me.

On December 2, 2006, the men at my church fixed breakfast for the women. My mother and I decided to attend. Judge P walked in. He started cleaning off the tables. He looked at me and smiled, then he walked over and wanted to know how things were working out for me. I told him Judge M. T. Thompson Jr. bound me over to circuit court. He explained to me how to pick a jury. I thanked him for sharing that information with me.

My pastor eventually arrived, and my mother called him over and told him what happened to me. He asked me why I hadn't called him. I didn't respond. He then told me to call his secretary to make an appointment. He would like to meet with me Monday.

On December 4, 2006, I started working at a new GM facility located in Flint, Michigan. My transfer had come. I had prayed for the transfer. **"THANK GOD FOR ANSWERED PRAYERS."** I don't have to see the Holland Road Exit again.

December 8, 2006, 3:30 P.M., I met with Pastor J. I shared with him a little bit of what happened to me. He interrupted me saying, "They threw 'YOUR ASS' in jail as if you were a black male?" He started to laugh, as if my situation was a joke. I didn't like the way he interrupted me. I looked at him stone-faced, and he put his hand over his mouth and said, "Oops." I started back sharing what happened to me and talking about how M. T. Thompson Jr. allowed the prosecutor to threaten me in the courtroom. He shared with me he knows M. T. and that his father was a minister. He knew the father on a personal level, and he had a few brief encounters with Judge M. T. Thompson Jr.

Pastor J had his secretary call Foss Avenue Baptist Church to set up a meeting with Pastor Emeritus Roosevelt Austin. Once he got off the phone I asked who Pastor Austin was. He shared with me Pastor Austin was a retired pastor out of Saginaw, Michigan. He was a strong believer in equal rights. He asked if I could return to his office the following Friday at 3:30 P.M. "Yes," I answered.

On December 15, 2006, 3:30 P.M., Pastor Emeritus Roosevelt Austin was there and I was there, but we were informed by the pastor's assistant that he was not able to meet with us. No reason was given and that she would be taking notes and sitting in on the meeting. I didn't have a problem with her sitting in on the meeting since my late uncle, Dr. Stanley Turner by marriage, was also her maternal uncle. It would have been nice if I had been informed of this change beforehand. I found it kind of rude to Pastor Emeritus Austin, who took the time out of his busy day, to come and share in this meeting. I'm not a member of his congregation, and he doesn't know me, but he was here. I wondered if it was because I am a female and a blue-collar worker and that is why Pastor J didn't bother to show up. His assistant didn't give a reason.

We followed her to a room with a big conference table, where I shared with Pastor Emeritus Roosevelt Austin about what happened to me. He asked me how long I had been employed with GM. I answered 26 years. He replied, "Oh, I know you weren't acting a fool going to work." He read the police reports. I told him I did not use all that profanity, and I told him how M.T. Thompson Jr. allowed the prosecutor to threaten me in the courtroom and how he bound me over for trial. I explained nothing was wrong with the light over my license plate. He asked me if I had proof, and if so, he would like to see it. "Yes, I do, but my attorney has it," I replied.

He asked for my attorney's name and number, which I gave to him. I let him read the ending of my prelim trial. After reading it, he took both his hands and hit the table in disbelief. He said in a loud voice "THAT M. T. Thompson Jr. **KNEW THAT BOY WAS LYING!!!**" (Jose Douglas) He told me he couldn't promise me anything, but he knew the judge I would be standing before, Judge William Crane, and he was going to talk to him on my behalf. He also said Buena Vista was dirty and make sure I sue them. I promised him I would. We shook hands, and the meeting was adjourned.

On December 23, 2006, a childhood friend was having a 50th birthday party. I really didn't want to go, but my friends told me I needed to get out of the house, so I decided to go. I had a wonderful time seeing classmates. It reminded me of happier times. I didn't share with anyone what I was going through, but it was hard.

January 2007. I was excited for the New Year. The one thing I noticed was that my uncle RJB seemed to be happy about my situation. He stood behind me while I was bowling and made fun of my bowling. I have a high backswing that he doesn't agree with, but he has three children, two females and two males, two grandsons, one granddaughter, one great-granddaughter, and none of them bowl. If he needed to teach someone how to bowl, he should have taught one of his offspring. I don't bowl on his team, nor does he pay for my bowling. This man has never been kind to me. When I was a child, he made fun of the way I looked. He called me Olive Oyl from the cartoon "Popeye" or Skinny Minnie. He tormented me my whole childhood with his verbal abuse, and this false arrest made him happy. When I missed a ten pin, he made a noise like a racing engine driving by. He called it a drive-by. I have repeatedly asked him to leave me alone. But he refuses.

Sometime in January my team was bowling his team. He anchored for his team; Tex anchored for my team. Tex bowled a 299. My uncle bowled 166. I bowled 167. He was upset at Tex so he took it out on me. He told me I was voted most likely not to succeed by my classmates and I succeed at nothing. He looked at me angrily but was not man enough to say anything to Tex. I looked at him, and I told him I succeeded at something: **"I BEAT YOU!!!!"**

"NO, YOU DIDN'T!!!" HE HOLLERED.

One of his teammates said, "Yes, she did. She beat you by one pin." You could have fried an egg on his head he was so upset.

You would think that a relative would have your back when you are going through a crisis, but not this uncle. It's like he's from the planet Mars. He loves to demean his family. If I was a daughter of one of his golfing or bowling buddies, he would be defending me, but since I'm a relative, he's at home sitting at his kitchen table attacking my character without asking what happened. I try to stay away from this man. I don't need his negative comments when I have to fight the fight that GOD has placed before me, but I had to remember, the devil is busy and he's working through my uncle. He will send anyone to try to steal, kill, and destroy. He doesn't care who he is using. But GOD has something for me at the end of this race. He's nothing but a hurdle that I have to jump over.

I was happy it was my birthday, February 11, 2007. I got a gift that I didn't expect. I cosigned for a car for my oldest niece that I loved with all my heart. One ex-boyfriend told me if I loved him like I love my niece, we would be married with a house full of kids. I will admit I spoiled her. All she had to say was **"I WANT!!"** and I'd try to get it, no matter the cost, if I had to eat Bologna sandwiches to pay for it. I would! My oldest sister, the late Krystal Davis-Wright, warned me to take off my rose-colored glasses and see the true person. I refused to do that. One of my friends warned me that she was ungrateful. I was very upset at this friend. I told her to mind her own business, that this was my niece, and I could do whatever I wanted to do for her. It was none of her business.

So I decided to cosign for a 2004 red Saturn for my niece that told me she would not disappoint me—and I fell for it. My niece decided, for reasons unknown to me, she no longer wanted the car and just gave it back to me in bad condition. The interior of the vehicle smelled like sour milk, and the seats were stained. It had just enough gas to get to the gas station. I was having a hard time understanding why my niece would do this to me. I'm the reason she had her job. I read in the newspaper that my cousin's (Bob) place of employment was accepting applications, so I drove to his home. He wasn't there. His wife was home, so I explained to her why I came by. She told me he had the referral, but he promised it to someone else, but, she said, family comes first. She handed me an application, and I filled it out and placed my telephone number on it, and signed my niece's name. Soon, the plant called my home. My niece was hired.

November 2006. My niece never paid me a car note since she became employed. My friends were upset, but I was not. I didn't pray before I made this decision. I was disappointed but not upset. I held my niece to a standard that she couldn't live up to. Matthew 18:27 says, "Then the lord of that servant was moved with compassion, and loosed him, and forgave him of the debt."

My mother called me telling me she wanted me to call my uncle RJB, the uncle I feel hated me. She explained to me that he was the head of our family with the loss of my great-uncle Oscar Woodson. We were supposed to go to him when there was a family dispute. I listened to her, but I didn't believe he was capable of not being biased when it came to me. She kept talking, telling me to call him and set up a meeting with him, my niece, and myself. She felt it was heavy on me paying two car notes, plus insurance and having to go to court in May of 2007. She asked me to call him the next day, so I finally told her I would do it!!! Maybe there was something she saw in him that I didn't see. All I saw was evil and bitterness.

The next day after work I sat in my car. I looked at my cell phone for a few minutes, trying to figure out if I should call him or not. I decided I would call, so I dialed his number. My heart was beating rapidly. He answered the phone. When I heard his voice I hesitated. I finally got the words out.

"Hello, Uncle RJB, how are you?"

He answered, "Fine, what do you want?" he asked.

I asked him if he would be a mediator between my niece and me. I explained to him the situation. He answered me so nasty, "What makes you think I want to get in your mess? What makes you think I know how to get in touch with your niece? I need to speak to my wife. She might not want me in your mess. You call me back tomorrow," then he slammed the phone down on me.

I stared at my phone in disbelief. How can this man be so evil toward me???? I never did anything to him but treat him with respect. I would not waste my time with this man any longer. I would not call him tomorrow. I have patterned my life after his mother, Lenora Black. She was always a lady. She and her Blue Star Mothers showed me how to live a Christian and a ladylike life. I will always be grateful to those ladies for showing me the way. Then my thoughts turned to my uncle. I remembered when his place of employment, AC Spark Plug, a division of General Motors, was hiring in 1976. Everybody wanted to work there. The work was fast and easy. You had to have a referral from someone who worked there, though. My older sister and I heard about it. We drove over to his home to see if he would give her and me a referral. He looked at me and asked, "Oh, you want to work?"

I replied, "I already have a job, but, yes, I would like to find a job that pays more money."

He took a bite from his banana and said he had given his referrals away to his daughter's best friend's brothers and walked away toward his bedroom.

I needed to change the mood. I was beginning to feel hatred toward this man.

Don't you at least check with your family before you give it away to an outsider? And, of course, one of the young men was hired.

To change the mood, I started to look through my CD case and I found Frankie Beverly and Maze, **"HAPPY FEELINGS"**!!

Later on that evening my mom called me and asked if I had spoken to my uncle. I answered yes. She asked, "Will there be a meeting between the three of you?"

I answered no. I then asked her to tell me something nice about her brother. She answered when she was having a rough time, she was on sick leave and her money was cut off, he sent his wife over with meat and vegetables and told her if she needed money to call. I said, "Okay, has he ever been nice to me?"

"Yes," she replied, "when you were a toddler, he bought you and your cousin Shelia velvet dresses." Mine was blue, and Cousin Shelia's was red. He placed us in the backseat of his car and took us around to visit the family. He loves babies.

I told her, "Thank you for sharing this with me. I needed to know that he had some good in him toward me even if I was just a baby."

May 2007. I had to go to Saginaw, Michigan, to stand on the charges Judge M. T. Thompson bound me over to the circuit court for. My best friend Tonnie J drove from Detroit to go to court with my mother and me. My appointment time was 9:00 A.M.

We sat in Judge William Crane's courtroom where they called everyone except me. It was now 11:30 A.M. My attorney walked over to the court reporter and asked why I hadn't been called. She replied she didn't have my records. He made her go through all the files on her desk. My file was not there. He was upset. He told her I took the day off work, and he arranged his caseload so he could be here, so what's going on??

She replied, "I don't know."

He walked over and told me I could leave. Once again, sabotage in Saginaw!!!!

As we got up to leave, he assured me it wouldn't happen a second time. I asked, "Do you think Judge M. T. Thompson Jr. is playing games?"

He answered, "No, I don't think he would do anything like this."

Once my mother, Tonnie J, and I were on the elevator, my mother pushed #3. I said, "Mom, what are you doing???"

She replied, "I want to show Tonnie J the man I was going to fight."

I asked, "Mom, do we have to go to that man's courtroom?"

She jumped off the elevator. Tonnie J followed her. I got off and followed both of them. I didn't trust my mother. She opened that door and went straight in Judge M. T. Thompson Jr.'s courtroom. She and Tonnie J just stared at him. I walked in to get them out of the courtroom, and then he saw me staring at him. I wore all yellow from head to toe. I didn't want him to notice me, but I was too bright for him not to notice me, so I waved at his court reporter and pulled both of these women out of his courtroom. As we were walking toward elevator, my mother was sharing with Tonnie how she wanted to whop him upside his head with her purse. Tonnie J was laughing at her, and I'm begging Tonnie J to stop before she turned into Aunt Esther from the sitcom *Sanford and Son*. I treated both of them to lunch in Frankenmuth. Frankenmuth calms me down, and Christmas is my favorite time of the year.

Now it was the middle of May. Tonnie J drove from Detroit to go to court with me. Just she and I were at the courthouse this time. The same thing happened again. Everyone was being called except me. My attorney approached the court reporter. She told him to calm down, that she was going to call me. It was 11:20 A.M. before they called me. I had been there since 9:00 A.M. Once I was called, my attorney was arguing for a motion for the charges to be dismissed, but the prosecutor was not having it. We were given another date for July 2, 2007.

As my attorney and I were walking toward the elevators, he was trying to explain to me the motion he was submitting to the Judge Crain. Once on the elevator, he hit #3. We got off the elevator, and he handed me the motion. I started to read the motion. After I finished, I said to him, "About time!!" In the motion something was said about the prosecutor threatening me. My attorney explained to me that you play your cards when it's to your advantage. He pointed at Judge M. T. Thompson Jr.'s courtroom and said I really didn't understand him at all. I replied, "He doesn't have a heart, brain, or courage." He just smiled, and I left.

STATE OF MICHIGAN
IN THE CIRCUIT COURT FOR THE COUNTY OF SAGINAW
PEOPLE OF THE STATE OF MICHIGAN vs. KIM R. DAVIS, Defendant
LAW OFFICES OF FRANK and FORSTER, P.C.
THOMAS L. FRANK (P13638), Attorney for Defendant
602 Hancock, Saginaw, Michigan 48602, Phone: (989) 790-5917
Case No. 06-028329-FH 0607074

HON. WILLIAM A. CRANE
MOTION TO DISMISS WITH LEGAL AUTHORITY
Defendant, by her attorney states:

1. She was arrested by Jose Douglas, a patrol officer for the Buena Vista Police Department on September 28, 2006, at 23:48 hours.

2. A warrant for her arrest was authorized by the Prosecutor's Office on September 29, 2006, for Fleeing—4th Degree, contrary to MCL 257.602a (2).

3. Defendant, on October 13, 2006, appeared for preliminary examination at which time the charges were dismissed.

4. On October 13, 2006, the Saginaw County Prosecutor's Office reissued another complaint against Defendant charging her with fleeing—3rd Degree, contrary to MCL 750.479a(3), and Resisting and Obstructing a Police Officer, contrary to MCL 750.81(d).

5. On November 9, 2006, Defendant appeared for arraignment and demanded a preliminary examination within 14 days, it being scheduled, and held on November 15, 2006.

6. At the October 13, 2006, preliminary examination, the prosecution offered to allow the Defendant to plead to a 1-year misdemeanor of attempt Fleeing—3rd degree. Defendant declined. The assistant prosecutor then said to her that they were unable to proceed (no witness), and if she didn't take the deal or consent to adjourn the preliminary examination, they would reissue the more serious offense of Fleeing—3rd Degree.

7. Not only did they reissue Fleeing—3rd Degree, they tacked on Resisting and Obstructing a Police Officer.

8. The prosecution, by its actions and statements, violated the precepts set forth in United States vs. Goodwin, 457 US 268, which, in pertinent part, states:

There are two types of prosecutorial vindictiveness, presumed vindictiveness and actual vindictiveness. Actual vindictiveness will be found only where objective evidence of an expressed hostility or threat suggests that the Defendant was deliberately penalized for his/her exercise of a procedural, statutory, or constitutional right.

See also North Carolina vs. Pearce, 395 US 711, and People vs. Goeddeke, 174 Mich App 534, which says it is a violation of due process to punish a person for asserting a protected statutory or constitutional right. And to punish a person because she has done what the law allows is a due process violation of the most basic sort. Bordenkircher vs. Hayes, 434 US 357.

And finally, vindictive prosecution has resulted in a reversal of a manslaughter conviction where a Defendant insisted on a trial on the original charges of four (4) misdemeanors where the Prosecutor dismissed them and reissued manslaughter charges arising from the facts of the same misdemeanor charges. Thiqten vs. Roberts, 468 US 27.

9. Officer Jose Douglas stated at the preliminary examination that the only reason for the stop was because the registration light was out.

10. The registration light was not out. The Defendant's vehicle, a 2005 Pontiac Grand Prix, was at all times pertinent hereto in compliance with all equipment requirements. (See Exhibit A.)

11. The stop was pretexual and without the legal right to interfere with Defendant's liberty.

12. The Court at the preliminary examination refused to bind Defendant over on Count If Fleeing 3rd Degree. An appeal by the prosecution was never perfected.

13. Assuming for the moment that the registration plate light was out, this is merely charges against her by order quashing the complaint against her and discharging the bond.

14. That the Police Officer was without legal authority to remove Defendant from her vehicle.

15. That there is no underlying crime for which one can be charged with Resisting and Obstructing a Police Officer who was performing his duties as set forth in MCL 750.81d(1).

16. That the Police Officer's duty in this case was to write her a citation for defective equipment while she remained secure in her car, rather than searching her and her car.

WHEREFORE, your Defendant prays that this Court dismiss the charges against her by order quashing the complaint against her and discharging the bond.

Date: 5-30-07

Superior. Pontiac Cadillac 1717 South Dort Highway

Flint, Michigan 48503

Phone: (810) 744-1000 Fax: (810) 744-1077

Kim Davis

Year 2005

38276W Pontiac Grand Prix

Description of Service and Parts

#1 – 172: Trim Concern

She was given a ticket for design of Rear License Lamp Caused by Inspected Vehicle, both bulbs are working, tail lamp is a design of GM and operation to factory specs.

Work Performed by service (888) 0.00hrs @ 00.00

Subtotal: Labor: .00   Parts: .00   Total: .00

July 2, 2007. My best friend Tonnie J is here to ride to court with me. She smiles at my red Saturn, the one my relative gave back. I ordered seat covers off the Internet, purchased some rims and tires, and tinted the windows. I call it the "pimp mobile." I told her we are riding in the pimp mobile. She complimented my ride.

We went inside my place for some reason. I was messing around, and she kept telling me, "Come on, Kim, we're going to be late."

The telephone rang just as we were leaving. She told me not to answer the phone, but I did anyway. It was my attorney!! He said, "Kim, I have some news for you—"

Before he could finish, I became upset. I was thinking, he's calling to tell me the court has canceled my appointment. He said, "Calm down, Kim, **YOUR CASE HAS BEEN THROWN OUT OF COURT!!!!**"

I started screaming!!!! **"THANK YOU, JESUS!!!!!"** I screamed to Tonnie J, "IT'S OVER!!!!!!"

She started crying, saying, **"THANK YOU, JESUS!!!!"**

I started singing "Trouble in my way, I have to cry sometimes, I know that Jesus will fix it after while!!! Buena Vista in my way, I had to cry sometimes, I know that Jesus will fix it after while. Judge Thompson in my way, I have to cry sometimes, I know that Jesus will fix it after while!!!" After singing and praising the Lord I shared with Tonnie J how Judge Thompson's campaign manager, Pastor Emeritus Austin, ran interference for me and how awesome GOD IS!!! That he allowed the same man to run a campaign for me as he did for Judge Thompson to prove my innocence.

Tonnie J asked me if I would call my pastor. I told her, "Yes, out of respect I will call the church. He did introduce me to Pastor Emeritus Roosevelt Austin. Technically, he did nothing other than that. I didn't get a prayer or telephone call to check on my mental state. He never once asked the church to pray for me, but GOD always has a ram in the bush."

My mother shared with her church Sunday school class my situation; she's a member of Mount Olive Baptist Church, pastored by the late Pastor Roy I. Greer. They immediately started praying for me. Three women from my mother's Sunday school class prayed for me morning, noon, and night. I called them my praying mothers. I called my mother at her place of employment and shared the good news. Then, Tonnie J and I drove to Foss Avenue Baptist Church looking for Pastor Emeritus Roosevelt Austin. He wasn't there for me to thank him for everything he had done for me. So we hit the highway to Pontiac and Detroit instead of calling my friends to tell about the good news. We wanted to share with them in person later that evening.

Finally, we arrived back in Flint. Tonnie and I stopped over at Frankie G's new home. He gave Tonnie J a tour of his home. We went to the basement and started listening to Mahalia Jackson's "Precious Lord, Take My Hand." I was beginning to cry, thinking about my grandmother, the late Lenora Black. Tonnie J was thinking about her late grandmother. Frankie G was thinking about his late mother.

After we dried our tears, I decided to have a victory party. I couldn't figure out where to host it. Frankie offered his home. I thanked him and told him I would rent a tent to keep traffic out of his home. I decided to have it on Sunday, August 26, 2007. The reason I chose Sunday ("Grooving on a Sunday Afternoon" by the Young Rascals in 1967) was it was one of my favorite songs growing up.

A friend of the family called me about what attorney I selected for the civil suit. I told him I had not selected an attorney yet, then he named one attorney, L F, and I said, "Oh yes! I've heard of him. We attend the same church." I told him I would call and make an appointment. The appointment was set for Monday, July 9, 2007. I was excited to see him. I'd heard so much about him. He drove a two-seater white Mercedes with a personalized license plate, was well dressed, handsome, and a ladies' man.

It was the day of my appointment. I had been calling my girlfriends all day, sharing with them my excitement of meeting this lawyer. It was 2:50 P.M. My shift ended, so I ran to the locker room to brush my teeth, take a quick shower, and change clothes. I ran and jumped into my car. I only had 12 minutes to get to his office. I arrived with 2 minutes to spare. I noticed the famous white Mercedes parked there. I jumped out of my car, walking quickly. I opened the door. I loved his office. It was housed in a Victorian carriage town in the historical area of Flint.

As I walked in, his secretary greeted. She offered me coffee or water. I declined both. She showed me where to be seated, telling me the attorney would be with me shortly.

As I took my seat, my imagination began to run wild, with me visualizing dinner parties being held in this beautiful home. To the front of me was a drawing room. To the right of me was a beautiful winding staircase. I could imagine the lady of the house flowing down the staircase in a pastel-colored gown, coming to greet her guests, but before I could finish my thoughts, I heard my name being called from the top of the staircase. I liked the sound of his voice. I couldn't wait to walk up the staircase.

Once I was at the top of the staircase I saw him. He was wearing tan pants, a tan Burberry shirt with red stripes, and nice loafer shoes. He wore gold wire-rimmed glasses, nice-smelling cologne, and stood 5 foot 9 or 5 foot 10 and weighed approximately 190 pounds. He had wavy salt-and-pepper hair. I could tell he was very handsome when he was younger. He looked to be between 57–60 and was dark in complexion. He extended his hand. I reached for his hand, and we shook hands, then he led me to his office. Once inside his office, I noticed beautiful African art hanging on the walls.

Once I was seated, we discussed my case. He told me I have a good case. I handed him all my paperwork. He looked over it, and then once he finished reading the police reports, he asked me had I used all of that profanity. I replied, "No, I only used *asshole* and *jackass*." I explained to him how Judge M. T. Thompson Jr. allowed me to be threatened in his courtroom. He replied, "They used 1920 tactics in Saginaw, Michigan," and that he would look over my case and get back with me later. Before I left he asked me about our pastor. He couldn't seem to get in touch with him. I told him it was July, and that he takes the whole month off for vacation. He smiled and said he had forgotten that. We shook hands, and I left.

August 6, 2007. It was the first Sunday of the month. As I arrived at church, I saw a friend of mine in the parking lot. I stood outside and talked with him for a while. Then I realized I was missing service, so I told him bye. Once inside, I took a seat on the back pew between my aunt and the DJ I hired for my party. I started writing out my check for my offering. Next, I heard Pastor J speaking about a promotion in some type of Baptist Congress. He didn't feel as if he was worthy to serve under this individual. I wasn't able to hear the end of the conversation because, all of a sudden, I heard something in my left ear. I felt two hands on my shoulder. I turned to my left to see what was going on. As I turned to my left, I saw the pastor's personal nurse looking at me. I asked, "What do you want?"

She spoke to me in a very scolding voice. She asked me if I was going to file a civil suit against Buena Vista Police Department. I replied yes. She raised her voice and told me, "No, you're NOT!!!! Pastor sent me back here to tell you it's over and done with, and for you to move on!!!"

I replied, "I'm the one that spent 4 days in jail and $5,000 for attorney fees. I'm filing. I don't care what he thinks; he didn't support me anyway!!!"

She moved quickly away from me. I watched as she walked along the west wall of the church, heading toward the back of the pulpit. Once she arrived at the back, she whispered in Pastor J's ear. After she finished, he gave me a nasty look, reminding me of the look of Judge M. T. Thompson Jr. I looked back at him. After the choir finished with their selection, he got up and said, "When you're a member of a church, you're under your spiritual advisor, who is your intercessor between you and GOD. Who do you think you are to lean on your own understanding? When GOD brings you through something, who do you think you are to seek revenge on people???"

After he said, that I leaned over to my DJ and told him, "He's talking to me." I told him what his nurse said to me.

He said, "That's a civil rights case not a revenge case."

All while Pastor J was talking, my aunt was shouting, "Amen, amen!!!!"

I wanted to tell her to shut up!!! I started to leave, but changed my mind. I wanted to hear the sermon to make sure if I could be under his leadership. Needless to say, I didn't hear a word he said. My mind was made up. I was leaving because a house divided cannot stand. I was going to file my civil suit, and he didn't want me to. GOD is not a GOD of confusion. I must leave. GOD has been too good to me for me to bring division in his house. Two church members, one a deacon, male, and one female, came forth to give testimonies. I listened to the male. He was speaking of a surgery that he recovered from. He mentioned they had to perform the surgery through his neck. The female was speaking of overcoming cancer. They had wonderful testimonies. I was not one for getting up, speaking in front of crowds, but I was wondering why Pastor was trying to shut down my testimony.

As the church service ended, I watched him shaking people's hands and smiling at them. I wondered if these people truly needed him, would he treat them as he treated me?

Once inside my vehicle I started singing "Smiling Faces Sometimes," by The Undisputed Truth, with the line "beware of the pat on the back, it just might hold you back." I hoped the promotion Pastor received was on his own merit and not for shutting me down. I have work to do for my people in Buena Vista, Michigan. I have to fight this fight for the injustice of the police department not having cameras in their cruisers. This gives them an advantage to lie.

Once home, I called my mother to tell her about my former pastor. She listened to me, telling me I was upset, and she would call me back later to talk to me. I went for a run at Flint Hamady High School. After I finished my run, I drove to Frankenmuth and went to Bronner's Christmas display that calms me down.

Once home, I showered and dressed to meet my friends for dinner. The telephone rang. It was my mother. She explained to me she spoke with my two aunts who are members of my former church, and the three of them feel I should request a meeting with my former pastor, J, to understand his reasoning for this request of me not to file a civil suit.

I replied, "Mother, I don't care why he feels the way he feels. In my eyes, he's a coward. You don't send a woman to do a man's job. He wasn't man enough to call me into his office and speak to me in person. I didn't give him permission to share with his personal nurse or anyone else my personal business.

"As far as your two sisters go, they have a lot of nerve. They never once said anything to me about what I was going through. I sat on the same bench with them almost every Sunday, and they never said one word to me about my situation, didn't tell me they were praying for me. They acted as if it never happened to me. They treated me as if I went to Jamaica or the Bahamas for 4 days, not jail. There is no way I could have a family member that I know for a fact was on her way to work and end up in jail and not be concerned. I have never been arrested before. They have never seen me drunk or high on drugs. I have always been a lady in their presence, and for them to treat me the way they have, I could care less what they have to say, so as far as I'm concerned, they are just as coldhearted as he is. Furthermore, this is between GOD and me. He has the master plan. GOD doesn't give you a task and tell you to drop it. He selected me, and I'm going to finish it, Mom.

"My former pastor, J, doesn't want this because of Judge M. T. Thompson Jr. and his friendship with his late father. Mom, I have some scriptures to share with you, like 1 Thessalonians 5:21, 'Prove all things, hold fast that which is good.' Mom, I don't know how, but I must prove that Timothy Patterson is a bad cop, and I am not pressing for the mark of my ex-pastor, J. I'm pressing for the mark of the higher calling in Christ Jesus. Philippians 3:14 says, 'I can do all things through Christ who strengthens me.'

"Mom, I'm a runner. When I used to participate in road races, I never dropped out. There is one race I'd like to share with you. My friend Billy and I ran a race in Ypsilanti, Michigan. The race was called the 'spaghetti bender.' I arrived late to Billy's home. I had the time mixed up. Billy looked at his watch and said, 'Rose,' that's what he called me, 'we will probably get to the race late, but we will still run.' When we arrived at the race, everyone was gone.

"We ran inside, got our race numbers, and took off running. We made a left turn instead of a right turn, and one of the race officials had to come and turn us around in the right direction. That didn't stop us from completing the race. We ran the whole race, and we took pleasure in passing people. Each time we would pass someone we would give each other a high five. We would say we are pressing toward the next victim.

"Billy never left my side. I told him once we had caught up with the pack to go ahead. He said, 'No, we started together, and we will finish together.'

"Once we arrived at the finish line, my younger sister Kathy cheered us on. She couldn't believe we finished in the middle of the pack since we were late. That's how GOD is. He wants you to complete your mission, and he won't leave your side. Just as Kathy was cheering us on, the people in Buena Vista will cheer me on when I get cameras in the police cruisers. I'm not as young as I used to be, but I still have the same determination.

"Mom, get your Bible and turn to 1 Corinthians 9:24–26. It says, 'Know ye not that they which run in a race run all, but one receiveth the prize? So run, that ye may obtain.' Do you not know that in the foot-race the runners all run, but that only one gets the prize? You must run like him, in order to win with certainty. Don't you know that those who run in a race all run, but one receives the prize? Run like that, that you may win.

"Mom, my pastor is demeaning what happened to me because I'm a woman and I'm a blue-collar worker. He doesn't care that M. T. Thompson is an unjust judge."

My mother told me to turn to Luke, chapter 18 verses 1–8. We read it together, and yes, that's JUDGE THOMPSON!!!! I told Mom goodbye and said that I will call her tomorrow.

Monday morning and it's my 9:00 A.M. break. I called my attorney L F and shared with him what his pastor, J, wanted and said that it was unacceptable to me. I asked if he was still going to be my attorney. I explained I would be looking for a new church home.

He replied he would handle my case, that my civil rights were violated, but he wanted to know if he could ask his pastor, J, why he felt the way he did. I told him sure, but I didn't want to know.

August 24, 2007. I drove to Ann Arbor, Michigan, to pick up my three goddaughters. GOD never blessed me to marry and have children, but he showed me favor when these three young ladies entered my life. They have been exceptional daughters toward me: Shantal, Shakisha, and Shakayla. Their mother's nickname is So-So. She's been wonderful toward me too. She allowed me to discipline and love them. Sometimes I spoil them. She has no problem with my love for her children, which is rare. Sometimes parents become jealous, but she's a rare jewel.

August 26, 2007. It was my party. My girls and I loaded up my vehicle with food. We spent all day Saturday cooking. We barbequed chicken leg quarters, pork chops, polish sausages, hot dogs, and hamburgers. We made spaghetti, mac and cheese, coleslaw, and carved up turkey meat. My mom brought candied yams and potato salad. Tonnie J was bringing baked beans. My friend Marietta was bringing peach cobbler. Pierre Burnett, my friend from Indianapolis, was bringing soft drinks. My friend Marvin Horne was just bringing himself. I will never forget when he told me he would do anything for me. That's what a friend is for.

Homer Bond was in house. My godmother was bringing a pound cake. One of my aunts brought a peach cobbler. Frankie G had his greens on the stove cooking, smelling up the backyard. My brother-in-law J B brought me three large tables to set my food on. I was so excited!!!!

Once I arrived at Frankie G's home, the tent was set up in the driveway. It looked beautiful. I was excited. My goddaughters were getting tired of me singing "Groovin' on a Sunday Afternoon." I had sung that song from my house to Frankie G's home.

We immediately started setting up the food, but before I could finish, guests started arriving, congratulating me on my victory. I had guests from Saginaw, Detroit, Pontiac, Indianapolis, and Flint. It was a wonderful feeling to be loved!!! My DJ was playing smooth jazz. People were laughing and eating, just relaxing and enjoying themselves. No one was wanting for anything. My three goddaughters were waiting on my guests, fixing plates, bringing soft drinks.

My family members were here. My favorite cousin Juana Woodson was here. She had the "Woodson mystique." She made you feel loved and special, like her father, the late Marcus Garvey Woodson, and his brothers, Uncles Oscar, Renzellas, and Eddie Woodson, as well as my great-aunts, who were also special. Aunt Penny gave you wisdom. Aunt Adeline and Aunt Lillian made the best desserts. Their cakes melted in your mouth. My two aunts couldn't cook anything that wasn't good. But the one thing above all else that you received from the Woodsons was unconditional love. They treated you as if you were royalty.

As I looked at my cousin Juana, the thought ran across my mind that I should have asked her to bring some homemade rolls. She's just like her mother, the late Loraine Woodson. Oh, how I remember the Thanksgiving dinners in Detroit. You walked through the front door, and the aroma of GOOD FOOD would make you weak in the knees!! It was a blessing to be around so much love. Aunt Loraine cooked enough food for 50–60 people by herself, and everything was GOOD!!!! I would sit in the kitchen to catch the homemade rolls fresh out of the oven. My aunt Alma Lee would cook a big dinner on January 8th, just like Aunt Loraine, and her food was delicious. My victory party reminded me of those days. I blew a kiss to the sky in memory of my family members who have passed on.

My uncle that said I was voted most likely not to succeed at anything was not here. Neither he nor his family came. He was probably upset that I achieved victory in winning my case, so now he couldn't sit at his kitchen table and gossip about me. But it hurt my feelings that his two daughters didn't show. I had always supported them in their endeavors.

My lifelong friends Deb W and Servella made it. I was so happy to see them. As one of my guests prepared to leave, I walked her to her vehicle. She had a different vehicle, so I asked her when she bought it. She replied she had been in an accident on her way to Georgia, with her grandchildren in the backseat. She rolled over several times on 1-75 in Ohio. She had just gotten back, and she wanted to come and share with me. We praised **GOD** for her safe return, and that she and her grandchildren were not harmed. As I walked back to my party, I **THANKED GOD** for her friendship, that she was willing to come to my victory party in spite of what she had been through and gave

Police, Lawyers & Judges

me $7, because that's God's number. I am truly blessed. I know I'm blessed.

Then I saw my three praying mothers from Mount Olive Baptist Church, Princess, Lolanda, and Nina Jones. Having the three of them pray for you is like running a relay. Princess starts it off, hands the praying baton to Lolanda, and you save the best for last with Nina Jones running anchor. Carl Lewis, Flo-Jo, or Jesse Owens couldn't run down the prayers that she sends up.

As my party came to an end, I walked into the kitchen to wash dishes, and Frankie G informed me my little cousin Melissa had cleaned the kitchen. He told me she's a dishwashing diva. I could only praise **GOD** again. As I left, I hugged Frankie G for allowing me to use his home.

On September 9, 2007 at 3:00 P.M., my friend Arlene called me and shared with me that today was Member Loyalty Day at my former church. Her brother Pastor R. Turner from Evansville, Indiana, was the guest speaker today. He's the late Pastor Emeritus Brady's grandson. They had a special service for the person with the longest membership. She informed me that my name was called. I had the oldest membership with 40 years, and that they had a gift for me. She asked me if I was sure I wanted to change my membership.

"Yes," I answered, "don't you understand that was a setup? He figured I would be there today because your brother preached. He knows you and I are friends. He's never acknowledged me before. He's always given this honor to a nurse that left the church as a teenager and broke her membership, then she returned in 1989. I remember giving her the right hand of fellowship. I was ushering that evening for the thirtieth church anniversary. He gave her a chauffeured limousine. This is nothing but a ploy to stop me from filing a civil suit, and he thinks whatever gift he has for me will stop me later, thanks to his games and gifts. I'm joining my church next week."

"Oh, Kim!!!!" she said. "Are you sure??? You are just going to give up 40 years??"

"Yes, I am," I replied. "Maybe the Lord will bless me to be with my new church 40 years."

Sunday, September 16, 2007, I joined my new church, Word of Life Christian Church. Our motto is: "Where the Word is alive and lives are changed." This is a church where everybody is somebody. My pastor, George Wilkerson, repeated this scripture, 1 Corinthians 15:58:

"Therefore, my beloved brethren, be ye stedfast, **UNMOVEABLE**, always abounding in the work of the Lord, forasmuch as ye know that your labour is not in vain in the Lord." The scripture means, to me, to finish my race. It doesn't matter if you are a billionaire or a ditchdigger. He treats everyone the same. He's about saving souls, not your bank account or where you work. We are all about GOD'S work.

September 20, 2007. My mother called me regarding the Jena Six march held in Louisiana. Michael Baisden and Rev. Al. Sharpton led the march. She informed me when one of the young men's father was talking to Reverend Sharpton that his pastor wouldn't support him. Reverend Sharpton replied, "Don't go back in that church. Find you a minister that is willing to support you." She apologized to me for telling me to talk to my former pastor. I wondered, if it were six teenage girls, would it have drawn so much attention?? Maybe I'm just feeling this way since all the black men have treated me harshly concerning my injustice.

I was stunned by the telephone call I received. It was my cousin from Pontiac, inviting me to her party. She didn't support me at my victory party. Instead, she offered all kinds of excuses why she couldn't support me. Now I was wondering why it took her 6 weeks to call to inform me of this, and I don't believe her. She wanted me to come to her birthday celebration. I was not going. My friends supported me, but she and her family chose to ignore me. She never called me to lend support when I was going through my situation. I thanked GOD for my friends. Proverbs 18:24 states, "A man [that hath] friends must show himself friendly." One thing that I love about life: you inherit your family, but GOD allows us to choose our friends. We get to go to the garden and pick out the best fruit and vegetables in that garden and claim them as our friends, but we must also be the best friend that we can be, so choose your friends wisely and love them unconditionally. There is a friend [that] sticketh closer than a brother or cousin; it's the Father, Son, and Holy Ghost. I didn't know when I was younger singing the hymn, "Oh what a Friend we have in Jesus," just how true it was. He's been a friend to me, showing me unconditional love, for without GOD, nothing is possible!!!!

Police, Lawyers & Judges

October 21, 2007. It was Women's Day at my former church. My friend Arlene and her mom were singing in the Women's Chorus. She called to inform me my lawyer was at church. I asked her how she knew who he was. She told me my former pastor had him stand up and give Sister C $50 for her eightieth birthday. I replied, "He got up and did this?"

She answered yes. I told her I need to find me a new lawyer. She asked me why I feel this way. "If he's telling him to get up and give people money, and he's doing it, that means the pastor is controlling the situation."

The next morning at my 9:00 A.M. break I called my attorney to check on my case. His voice had the sound of treason in it. He started telling me I cursed the police out. He said that I didn't do anything, that they stopped me for nothing because my paperwork proved I did nothing, but I went to jail because I cursed. However, cursing is only a ticket-worthy offence. You cannot go to jail for cursing. He recommended that I not file a civil suit. I replied, "You read the police reports when I first came to your office, and I told you I did not use all that language. **I TOLD YOU ALL I SAID WAS JACKASS AND ASSHOLE!!!** And I will be filing a civil suit with you or without you!!!!"

He replied, "You're still filing a lawsuit after what I just told you?"

"**YES, I AM!!!!** You're entitled to your opinion."

"Wait a minute, Kim, wait!!!! Let me see if I can get a co-counsel in Bay City, Michigan. That's where the federal court is located. Maybe I can get someone to work from Bay City. They know the ins and outs of Bay City, and I'll handle the Flint part of things."

I told him okay, but once we ended our conversation, I didn't think what he wanted was going to fly. It sounded as if he wanted to do the case, but his pastor didn't want him to. I'm not sure, but I think he's the lawyer for the church.

The following Monday I called. He told me to come get my paperwork. He couldn't find anybody to work with him. I immediately called Arlene and told her of his decision. We started laughing.

The following Sunday I was walking out of church and my pastor stopped me, asking me if there's anything he could do for me.

I replied yes, so he gave me his cell phone number and told me to call. I called, and we set up a meeting. I informed him of my situation and that I needed a lawyer. I showed him the paperwork and told him I didn't do all of that cursing, but I owned up to what I said. He just smiled at me. I told him I already asked the Lord for forgiveness. He informed me that we had a lawyer that was a member, and he would relay my situation to him, and if he couldn't help me, then he would refer me to someone who could. We ended our meeting with prayer. I met with the lawyer from my church. Civil suits were not his thing, but he had a couple of names for me. One was a woman, and one was a male, which captured my attention. I asked if he was African-American. He replied, "Does it matter?"

"**YES!!!** If he's an African-American named David Robinson, I want him!!!"

"I guess that's your lawyer because he's African-American."

"Oh, by the way, where is he located?"

He replied, Southfield, Michigan. I was ready to leap up in the air with excitement. The David Robinson I knew was kind, compassionate, helpful, a good friend, and a man of GOD. I will always remember him singing **"I SURRENDER ALL."** He passed away in 2004. I wasn't able to attend his funeral because I was on vacation at the time of his death. I felt **GOD** was sending him back to me, just like David in Acts 13:22, "And when he had removed him, he raised up unto them David to be their king; to whom also he gave their testimony, and said, I have found David the son of Jesse, a man after mine own heart, which shall fulfill all my will." I told everyone David was not dead, that he was going to be my lawyer!! This was the first time I didn't pilfer my decision. I had been trusting and leaning on **GOD**, and he never failed me. Now, I was taking over the situation. I believed David was a man after **GOD'S** own heart. He would be working in my favor. I knew to trust in GOD and not Man. This would be my downfall, for when you take your eyes off **GOD** you can't do anything . . . but **FALL!!!**

My cousin called January 15, 2008, and left a message concerning her parents' fiftieth wedding anniversary. I was shocked she was calling me. She was the daughter of my uncle that went out of his way to be mean and evil toward me. She left the date of the anniversary party,

May 17, 2008. I was happy I didn't have to go. I was bowling in a tournament on the 16th and 17th of May.

I called and made an appointment with Attorney David A. Robinson for February 14, 2008, at 3:00 P.M. When I met him, there was something about him I didn't like. He had a harsh tone, but I overlooked it because of his name. He was wearing a casual brown two-piece outfit, had a dark complexion, receding hairline, and stood about 5 foot 9 with a huge stomach protruding. He got up to make copies of my paperwork. He glanced over my papers like he was really concerned, then he asked me how long I had been working at GM. I replied, 29 years. Next, he asked how long I had been living at my residence, and I told him, 12 years. Then he questioned me about my credit. I answered, "My credit is just as good, or better, than yours. I have A1 credit."

Lastly, he asked if I had ever been in rehab. I replied, "No, I don't drink or do drugs. My pastor Emeritus Brady taught me as a young child that your body is a temple and I treat mine as such."

He told me I was every lawyer's dream, that a lot of people walk in his office that have a case similar to mine, but they didn't have the credit stability that I had, and they didn't have jobs. He said he would present my case to the other associates. I started telling myself this was a dream!!! I didn't know it would turn into a nightmare. When you don't consult with Jesus, that's all you will get—a nightmare in Southfield, Michigan.

February 15, 2008. My cousin called me again concerning her parents' anniversary. She left me a message that she needed help. I thought about how she didn't come to my victory party. She was invited. I thought of how her father antagonized me at the bowling center. I decided I was not going to answer her call. I got on my treadmill, and **GOD** started dealing with me. I thought about a song, "If I could help somebody along the way, then my living shall not be in vain." I thought of all the people that helped along my journey, and how, when my own church didn't support me, Mt. Olive Baptist Church supported me. I recalled how my family didn't support me, but my praying mothers and friends gave me nothing but love. At that moment, the telephone rang. It was the captain of my bowling team informing me that the dates were changed to the 15th and 16th, so I called and volunteered my services. My cousin told me what she needed.

ROBINSON AND ASSOCIATES, P.C.
Attorneys and Counselors at Law

David A. Robinson, Esq.

28145 Greenfield Road
Suite 100
Southfield, Michigan 48076-7116
Office: (248) 423-7234
Fax: (248) 423-7227
E-mail: darjd@earthlink.net

CONTINGENT FEE AGREEMENT

This agreement made this _14_ day of _February_, 200_8_ by and between _KIM ROSE DAVIS_ (client) and **Robinson & Associates, P.C.** (attorneys).

Where the client has a claim and cause of action for damages as the result of an incident, which occurred on or about _09/28/06 & 7/27/06_, and desires to employ **Robinson & Associates, P.C.** to prosecute said claim against those who may be responsible therefore.

Client engages and employs **Robinson & Associates, P.C.** to represent client and to prosecute the above claim and if necessary to file legal actions which the attorney deems necessary. Client agrees to pay attorney for services rendered pursuant to this agreement one third (1/3) of all monies and things of value recovered in said claim, whether by compromise, settlement or otherwise.

In addition to payment of our fees, you agree to reimburse us for costs advanced or out-of-pocket expenses we incur in representing you, such as filing fees, copying expenses, long distance telephone charges, computerized legal research charges, court reporter fees, witness fees, travel expenses, facsimile expenses, delivery charges, and the like. We reserve the right to request a retainer or withdraw as your legal counsel if we are not timely paid or for any other reason within our discretion, subject to any necessary court approval, without prejudice to our right to be paid for services rendered and costs advanced to that point. Similarly, you have the right to terminate our representation at any time, subject to any necessary court approval, but agree to remain responsible for costs and fees for work we have performed.

Any proceedings beyond those described, for example an appeal, will not be subject to the cap and may result in additional legal fees. If at any time you have any questions or concerns about your bill, you should call me to discuss your questions or concerns. It is very important to us that you understand all aspects of our representation, including our billing.

If no monies or things of value are recovered, client shall not be indebted to attorney for his services. The applicable percentages referred to above shall be computed on the net sum recovered after deducting from the amount recovered all disbursements properly chargeable to the enforcement of the action. Any such costs are to be paid by client and in the event the attorney advances costs, then client shall reimburse attorney regardless of the outcome of the controversy. Attorney shall have the right to associate with or to employ other attorney(s) in connection with their duties pursuant to this agreement.

Contingent Fee Agreement
page 2

Attorney may withdraw from this employment at any time upon giving client reasonable notice and any right or claim, if by attorney for services previously rendered shall thereby be established by agreement between client and attorney, or if agreement cannot be reached, then any fee dispute shall be submitted to the American Arbitration Association for its determination which shall be binding upon the parties and a lien shall be established.

Client acknowledges receipt of a copy of this agreement.

_____   _____
Client Signature   Attorney Signature

I told her I would help her with everything she needed. I helped her secure a venue.

March 16, 2008. My mother called, asking me if I had the *Flint Journal*. I told her no. She asked me to go to the store to purchase one. I asked, "Mom, is it that important?"

"Yes," she replied, so I went to the store and purchased the newspaper, then I called her back and asked her what she wanted me to read.

She told me to turn to A-6, the Local News Section, to the article titled "Stories of Triumphs and Trials Abound at Mentoring." As I scanned through the article, I read "Black Men for social change held at the Urban League of Flint." I almost fainted when I read **"THERE'S NEVER BEEN A GOOD TIME TO BE A BLACK MAN IN AMERICA SAID SAGINAW DISTRICT COURT JUDGE M. T. THOMPSON JR."** I called my mother in disbelief. She said, "Kim, if I had known he was here in Flint, I would have protested against him speaking. I would have walked back and forth in front of the Urban League with a sign reading **'M. T. THOMPSON JR. IS AN UNJUST JUDGE. GET HIM OUT OF MY CITY!!!'"**

"Mom, did you read, 'It's a good time to be a Black Male in America' that he didn't say 'Female'? Maybe that's why he didn't treat me fairly."

May 2008. My cousin and I took our mothers to Las Vegas for Mother's Day. When I returned, I heard from my lawyer that Theophilus Clemons, his associate, would be working with me. He would be handling my case. My grandmother on my father's side had a brother whose first name was Clemons. He was a kind man. The name Clemons meant a lot to me. Also, I felt I was on the right road!!! I loved the way Theophilus spoke. He spoke with authority, telling me to make sure I was forthright with everything I shared with him. He did not appreciate when clients lied to him.

May 17, 2008. For the fiftieth wedding anniversary party, I was running around picking up decorations. I made two big pans of mac and cheese, and my friend from Farmer's Market made a beautiful centerpiece for the party. I helped set up the fiftieth anniversary dinner, and it turned out wonderful. My uncle's wife came over and thanked me for all I had done. She had to drag my uncle over to thank me. He barely opened his mouth. He said thank you so low

I couldn't hear him. I overlooked his ignorance and told him, "You're welcome."

June 2008. I ran into a childhood friend. She was a member of New Jerusalem Full Gospel Baptist Church under the leadership of Bishop Odis A. Floyd, Rev. Bernice Haynes in Meijer's on West Pierson Road. She had heard about my situation. We started sharing how good the Lord was. Tears began to roll down my cheeks. She was watching me and listening to me, then when I finished, she asked me, "When is the book coming out?"

I responded, "I don't write books!!!"

She told me **GOD** has been too good to me for me to keep it to myself. She said I should be shouting from the rooftop. "But, Bernice, I'm not a writer!!!"

She told me let **GOD** lead me and pray on it. We hugged and said our good-byes. As I walked away, I murmured to myself, "I'm not writing a book." I felt unqualified. I'm not a writer or missionary or prophet. Why would **GOD** use me? There are so many people with outstanding credentials. Why would **GOD** use me??? I was not calling Reverend Bernice a liar, but I didn't see a book coming out of this situation.

A few weeks later, one Sunday morning while getting ready for church, the Rev. Otis Moss III of Trinity United Church of Christ of Chicago, Illinois, was on TV and stated, "When **GOD** has done something tremendous in your life, you are to share the goodness of **GOD** with other people." I got upset at this and turned off the TV. I felt he was trying to tell me I needed to write a book about my situation. I thought, *He doesn't know me. He needs to* **SHUT UP!!!**

Labor Day, 2008, I decided to visit my friends in Indianapolis, Indiana. That Sunday, I went to church with my friends. Their church name was New Beginnings Fellowship Church. Pastor Anthony Jackson was absent this particular Sunday, so the Youth Pastor, Corey Duncan, preached the message out of Genesis, chapter 12:1–2:

"Now the LORD had said unto Abram, Get thee out of thy country, and from thy kindred, and from thy father's house, unto a land that I will shew thee: And I will make of thee a great nation, and I will bless thee, and make thy name great; and thou shalt be a blessing."

After he gave us his text he set the tone for his message with the theme song from the *Fresh Prince*. Everyone knew the lyrics except me. All I knew was "Yo, homes smell you later!" He wanted us to know sometimes we have to shut people out of our lives to give birth to what **GOD** has ordained us to do. After the message, I went and talked to the young minister telling him I enjoyed his message and it would stick with me. He gave me a huge hug and told me, "May **GOD** bless you with what you have to do." I was stunned!!!! What was he talking about?? People were standing behind me waiting to speak with him, but I wanted to know what **GOD** had for me to do. I was not writing a book if that's what he's talking about.

On my drive from Indianapolis to Michigan, I was trying to figure out what **GOD** had for me to do.

The church bowling league started up. My uncle was his usual self—mean and nasty. I tried to ignore him, but he wouldn't allow me to. He stood behind me, making comments when I missed the ten pin, complaining about my backswing being too high, etc. I wanted to scream at him, **"SHUT UP!!!"** I got upset at myself for helping with his Fiftieth Wedding Anniversary Dinner. I was upset with myself for spending the amount of money I did on them, $100, and he was *still* a jerk. I couldn't understand where he got his demeanor from. His mother was as close to an angel as humanly possible. My grandfather passed away before I was born. After thinking about the situation, I realized I helped his daughter, not him, so I tried to overlook him, but it was hard.

I asked my mother to come observe her brother. She came over. He was on lanes 9 and 10; I was on 11 and 12. He missed two ten pins, back to back, one on each lane I missed one on lane 12. He made his noise and started smiling. I turned around and said, **"SHUT UP!!!!"** I told him, "I didn't bother you when you missed your pins back to back," so he wiped the smirk off his face.

Then I went and talked to my mother. I asked her, "Did you see your brother?"

She replied, "Yes, he looked like some silly juvenile playing a prank on his teacher," and then she left after seeing it.

On November 29, 2008, my cousin Shaun was playing the violin at South Flint Seventh Day Adventist Church, with Pastor Melvin

S. Santos. The topic of the sermon was "The Purpose of Suffering." The scriptures used were 1 Peter 4:7–9, Romans 5:2–5, and Revelation 7:12. He said, "Amen: Blessing, and glory, and wisdom, and thanksgiving, and honour, and power, and might, [be] unto our God for ever and ever. Amen." Then he said, (1) After you suffer and make it through, you are to give glory to **GOD**, (2) Produce fruit, (3) Silence the devil to make us like Jesus, and (4) Enlarge our ministries toward others.

As I was listening, I started asking the Lord, "Am I really supposed to write a book?" When I came home after service, I asked the Lord to lead and guide me if I was supposed to write a book. *Let your words permeate my heart, and let my hands write what you want me to write.* I waited for the Lord to give me a sign.

The following Saturday, it was time for me to bowl in my church league. I was having a wonderful time. My sister-in-law was bowling with me. My friend Brenda was also bowling. We were acting like little kids. I didn't know if we were winning or losing; the fellowship was just wonderful!! As usual, here's comes my uncle. I missed the ten pin. He made his usual noise. This time I became angry, and I shouted at him, **"YOU MISSED TWO TEN PINS. I DIDN'T BOTHER YOU, SO LEAVE ME ALONE!!!!!** Do you know what you are??? You are a pathetic excuse for an uncle." He walked away. Good, that's what I wanted, for him to leave me alone.

A few people thought I was too harsh on him, so I asked them, "Didn't you hear him harassing me??"

"Yes," they replied, "but you're better than him."

I meditated on that during my drive home. I hopped on my treadmill, and when I finished with my workout, I showered and changed clothes, then I started reading the Bible. I turned to Ephesians 4:29, 31–32: "Let no corrupt communication proceed out of your mouth, but that which is good to the use of edifying, that it may minister grace unto the hearers. Let all bitterness, and wrath, and anger, and clamour, and evil speaking, be put away from you, with all malice: And be ye kind one to another, tenderhearted, forgiving one another, even as God for Christ's sake hath forgiven you."

After reading these scriptures I called my mother to ask her to talk to her brother. I explained to her the situation. I told her **GOD** has something for me to do, and her brother is trying to block me. I needed for him to stay away so I can complete my mission that **GOD** had sent me on. She told me she will go speak to him concerning this matter. I explained to her he's always been nasty, but he had turned up his assault on me since my jail experience. She said, okay, she would deal with it. I thought about my uncle. I realized the devil was using him, like when he would tease me as a child, telling me I looked like Olive Oyl from the cartoon "Popeye the Sailor Man" that began in 1954. I wouldn't speak. I was afraid of people. I felt ugly and unworthy. I understood the devil was trying to get those feelings back in me to stop the work that **GOD** had for me to do, but I was not that child anymore. I was going to bring it this time!!! Let the chips fall where they might. If people get their feelings hurt, oh well, so be it. **"THIS IS GOD'S WORK, NOT MINE."**

My mom called me back to inform me that she spoke with her brother. At first, he tried to act as if it was a joke, saying that everyone teased each other when they missed a ten pin. She told me she asked him if I teased him when he missed a ten pin. He answered no. He told her I was being too sensitive. She told him to leave me alone, and she wasn't playing. She said she didn't bother his children, and he wasn't going to bother hers. I had been through enough torment dealing with my situation.

December 26, 2008. I meditated and prayed and started writing my book. I wanted to give all the glory to **GOD**. He was the reason I made it over!!!!

Monday, December 29, 2008. I received a telephone call from David Robinson's administrative assistant. She informed me that my disposition was set for January 7, 2009, at Plunkett/Cooney Law Firm, 111 E. Court St., Flint, Michigan 48502. I was ready to tell my story. I wanted to see the lawyer Audrey Forbush. She sent a lot of paperwork for me to fill out, asking me personal questions pertaining to if I ever filed a civil suit before, information about my credit score, names of my supervisors, my work record, if I had been in rehab before, if I had been married. Had I been married, they wanted my ex-husband's telephone number to inquire about me.

I asked to speak to my attorney, who was David Robinson's associate partner. I wanted to know what he looked like. When we spoke, he started laughing, so I asked, "Why are you laughing? I've never seen you before. We've been communicating over the telephone the last seven months."

He replied, "I'm a big black guy, and I will be wearing a blue suit with a pink tie."

January 7, 2009. I drove to Plunkett/Cooney law firm, which is located downtown Flint (Chase Building) to give my disposition. My attorney, Theophilus Clemons, wasn't there yet. I waited patiently for him. As I was waiting, I prayed and asked **GOD** to give me strength and bless my memory. I was ready to get it on. My attorney finally arrived. He waved his pink tie at me. I smiled, and we shook hands, then we sat in the lobby for around 15 minutes, going over my disposition.

"One thing," he said to me, "bother me." He asked me, "Where were you going that night?"

I replied, "To work. You have all the paperwork. Didn't you read it?"

"No," he answered.

The opposing counsel was finally ready, so we went inside and sat at the round table. The opposing counsel was a Caucasian female around 5 foot 6 and 140 pounds. She had short blond hair and a beautiful smile. She offered me refreshments. I requested a bottle of water. Finally, the show was on the road.

I raised my right hand and promised to tell the truth, nothing but the truth, then I started telling my story. She listened to me and wanted to know how I knew the police officers' names.

"Easy," I told her. "It happened to me, and their names were on the police reports." I continued with my story. She interrupted me again, asking me what I wore to work that night. I told her I didn't remember. She told me I had on a gray jacket. I replied, "Maybe I did, I don't remember," then she asked me what I did every morning when I got off work. I answered, "Sometimes I work out; sometimes I go straight home, shower, and go straight to bed. It all depends on how I feel."

I started back, telling my story, and she interrupted again. She wanted to know where I got the $5,000 to pay for my attorney fees.

I looked her straight in her eyes and told her, "From **MYSELF!!!!**" She could tell by the way I answered I was upset. She told me she didn't mean any harm.

After I finished with my disposition, she reached across the table and shook my hand and told me she was sorry for what happened to me, then she said, "Are you writing about this?"

I didn't answer. I didn't understand her reasoning for the question. As my attorney and I were walking toward our vehicles, he said to me, "You sounded sincere and authentic."

I responded, "Of course, I did. I was telling the truth!!!"

He said, "People are going to think you're suing for retirement money because you have 29½ years."

I answered him, "They bothered me. I didn't bother them, and I really don't understand where you're coming from."

He said, "I'm going to settle this out of court, with your permission."

I was silent. I had no response. I didn't understand where he was coming from. We said our good-byes and that we would meet at the federal court in Bay City, Michigan, on the 17th of February.

Later, I received a phone call from Attorney Theophilus Clemons, telling me he wouldn't be able to come to the federal court in Bay City for the settlement hearing, that David A. Robinson would be there. I told him fine.

Friday, February 13, 2009, at 3:35 P.M., my cell phone rang. It was Attorney David Robinson. I answered my phone. He was rude, and he was slurping a drink in my ear while he's speaking to me. He asked me what I thought my case was worth.

I answered, "I don't understand what you mean."

"Give me a ballpark figure," he said.

I answered, "Three million dollars!!!"

He became irate, telling me, "**THEY WILL OFFER YOU TEN THOUSAND DOLLARS AND THROW YOU OUT OF COURT!!!** You call me back Monday when you have some time to think about it. I took you by surprise, so you call me back Monday." He took a big sip out of his drink and hung up.

I thought to myself, *I can't stand this man. He's rude and obnoxious, and I can't stand the sound of his voice. Yuck.*

Monday arrived. I didn't call that man.

Police, Lawyers & Judges

On Tuesday, February 17th, my mom was ringing my doorbell. She was excited about going inside a federal court. Upon our arrival there, we were greeted by three men, two Caucasian and one African-American. They looked to be between 60–70 years old, maybe retired police officers or some type of law enforcement. They checked our purses and keys as we walked through the metal detector. The African-American told us we wouldn't be there long. The judge was moving people in and out. "Don't expect to be any longer than 5 minutes."

We took a seat on a bench and waited for my attorney. Once my attorney arrived, I heard one of the men greet him, calling him by his name.

"DAVID ROBINSON, HOW HAVE YOU BEEN???"

He told the other two men he and David were police officers together. My heart dropped to my stomach. This man was a police officer? I had no respect for police officers. They were bullies with badges. I put my head down to my lap and thought, *Did I get in the bed with the devil???*

When Attorney Robinson walked over to where my mother and I were seated, I just stared at him. My mother smiled and shook his hand. He and I were staring at each other to see who was going to break the ice first. There was a BIG CHILL between us. I never spoke to him. He asked one of the men at the door if he and I could use a room. They showed us to a room, and the first question out of his mouth was, "Why didn't you call me like I told you to??"

Silence. I didn't answer him. I thought to myself, *I am not your woman or your wife that needs to answer you; plus you were rude when you slammed the telephone in my ear.*

He started talking about the case, telling me I couldn't get a fair trial in Bay City. I told him I could. He told me to get up and walk toward the door. I did. Then he told me there was nothing wrong with me, and that when you file a civil suit, people want to see you maimed, walking with a limp, or missing a body part. I told him I disagreed.

"Well, Kim, you work for General Motors, and people don't like General Motors workers. They feel they are lazy and overpaid. You saw what happened on Capitol Hill with the loan. Nobody wanted General

Motors to receive that loan, and when they see you, they're going to think about that loan and use it against you, and they won't like the way you look!!"

I answered him, "The workers at General Motors and myself, we pay taxes. Money is taken out of my check before I receive it. I don't care what you or anybody else thinks about us General Motor workers. We pay our fair share. We're not like you. We can't hide our money in tax shelters. As far as the way I look, I look like everybody else on this planet: an average female. I have two eyes, one nose, one mouth, two arms, and two legs; that's what everybody has."

Then I looked at him and asked, "Do you know how to present a case???"

He answered, "Yes!!!!" At that answer, I walked out of the room and sat next to my mother. He followed me, staring at me. I asked him, "What are you looking at??"

My mother asked me to be nice to him. I told her, "I will tell her about him on the drive home."

He asked me how I heard about him. I told him that a lawyer in Flint gave me two names. I selected him because of my deep admiration for the late David Robinson. I told him he had class and dignity. My mother started talking about how David meant so much in the Bible. He started smiling at my mother. She loved his name. It meant, "a man after GOD'S own heart." She and he started talking about David from the Bible, and I watched as he was posing like he was on the show titled *America's Next Top Model*. I will give him credit. He really knows how to pose standing against a wall.

A few minutes went by before the judge signaled for him and Opposing Counsel to follow him. I proceeded to follow them, but the judge told me, "No!" so I sat back down. They were only in the office for 5 minutes. Once he came out, we had to go to the federal court in Detroit. My attorney was happy about it. He knew the female judge. Her name was Judge Morgan. He made the statement, "She comes to everything." I started to ask him what he meant by that, but his telephone rang. He ended his call and informed me it was his private detective. I asked him if he ran a background check on Timothy Patterson and Jose Douglas. He answered no!!!

"Why are we here?" I asked. "If you haven't run a background check on them, what's the purpose of this visit here?"

He replied, "I'm going to get my 'private dick' to find out the dope on them."

This man was making me uncomfortable. Why in the world did he keep staring at me? He was leaning up against the wall, just staring, so I decided to stare back. He had on a blue pin-striped suit, white shirt, blue tie, blue shoes, and a black and white coat that was getting too small. He could barely fit it over his fat stomach. He wore a blue tam on his head. As we left the building, he was constantly talking about getting a new white BMW. My mother was trying to talk him into buying a General Motors product, but he said, "No, I have to have a BMW. Have you seen them?"

She answered no. Then the opposing counsel, insurance representative, Attorney Robinson, my mother, and I walked out of the federal court together. David stuck out his hand to my mother to shake her hand. She told him she didn't shake hands; she gave hugs, so they embraced. I just stood there and watched. Then he grabbed me, hugged me, and kissed me on the right cheek. I was livid!! You could have fried eggs on top of my head. It was the kiss of Judas I would later learn.

I received my paperwork from court to appear at United States District Court, Eastern District of Michigan, Southern Division, Thursday, March 26, 2009, at 10:00 A.M., before Magistrate Judge Virginia M. Morgan, room 651, 231 W. Lafayette, Detroit, Michigan 48226.

At the end of February I received a call from Tonnie J, telling me she just finished her disposition. She informed me they asked her a few times if I drank alcoholic beverages. She answered Audrey Forbush, "No! Kim's doesn't drink, neither do I!!!"

I said, "That's odd. She never asked me if I drank."

The first week of March I received a phone call from my other witness, Ms. Wilson. She told me Audrey Forbush gave her a hard time about me carrying dog spray. I asked her why. She answered, "She was trying to make something bad out of it, but I told her we get off work at different times of the night. It might be twelve o'clock, one o'clock, three or four o'clock. It doesn't matter. We need some type of protection with us. She seemed to have a problem with that." She told me they had her downtown Flint for 2–3 hours. I apologized for them keeping her that long. She answered, "No problem, that's what friends are for."

March 9, 2009. I called my attorney Clemons to inform him of the dog attacks in Buena Vista. As we were discussing it, he didn't understand why I felt it's important to my case. I faxed him a copy of the news article, informing him I would call him back on my next break.

At 11:30 A.M., during my break, I called and spoke with him again. He still didn't get it!!! **"YES," I TOLD HIM, "IT HAS A LOT TO DO WITH MY CASE. THEY TOOK ME TO JAIL FOR CARRYING DOG SPRAY AND CALLED IT A CONCEALED WEAPON!!!!** Don't you think if we use this article, it would make the police look like the idiots that they are, plus, if the lady and the man that were attacked had what I had on me, maybe they wouldn't have ended up in the hospital. You have this picture of a Buena Vista police officer on the front page with his Rock River AR-15 rifle being seen as a hero. Well, he's a bully with a badge. I have no respect for anyone who works for the Buena Vista Police Department."

"Well, Kim," he replied, "it doesn't have anything to do with your case!"

I was frustrated. I thought it did. Then we ended our telephone conversation.

March 26, 2009, 9:45 A.M. I walked into the United States District Court, Eastern District of Michigan, Southern Division, room 651, the courtroom of Judge Virginia M. Morgan. As my mother and I waited outside, David A. Robinson appeared in a black suit, black shoes, white shirt, black tie, a gray overcoat, and he was holding a manila folder in his right hand. He had a big smile on his face. I asked him immediately, "Where is Attorney Clemons?"

He answered, "He's out getting a disposition."

We made small talk until we were invited in by Judge Morgan's secretary. She showed us to a room with a large table with seating for eight people. As we sat down, I asked David, "Did you run the background check on the two officers?"

He answered, "I dropped the ball on that. Anyway, police get immunity in Michigan. They only have 3–5 seconds to make a decision so they get immunity." I was livid!!!! Just as I started to lash out at him for not running the background check, Judge Morgan appeared with Attorney Audrey Forbush and the insurance investigator. She was a Caucasian female, approximately 5 foot 3, who wore glasses and had reddish brown hair. She's definitely forgettable. She didn't stand out at all.

They asked my mom to leave the room. Judge Morgan offered me refreshments. I accepted green tea. After she gave me my tea, she turned and looked at me and told me she had some questions for me. She called me a "young lady." I didn't like that. I'm a grown woman. She said, "Young lady, I want to ask you about that language you were using. You called one officer a 'bitch.' You told one officer you were going to 'whoop his ass.' What do you have to say for yourself?"

I replied, "Everything you said was a lie!!! I had no reason to call anyone a bitch or tell a grown man that I was going to whoop his ass when I see him out somewhere. The first reason being, I don't live in that area. Second, I have transferred my job. Third, I committed no crime. I don't have a record. There were no drugs or alcohol on me. I was not speeding, and I feel you're being unfair. You have said nothing about me being called a 'crackhead' or a 'street woman' or anything about being locked up in a bathroom or slammed into a car."

At that moment, she turned and looked at Audrey Forbush and asked if there was a video of this. Audrey replied no. She asked her if I had a record. Audrey replied no.

I said, "Isn't that convenient that they can say I carried on like this with no evidence?"

At that moment, David Robinson put his right hand on my left hand and told me that's what he was here for, to plead my case, not me. At that point in time I froze, as if I were in a trance. I could hear what was being said, but I couldn't respond. Words wouldn't come out of my mouth. Audrey was lying about me, saying that I drove a mile before I stopped. David was lying. He said I was stopped for improper lane use. I tried to scream out, **"YOU'RE A LIAR. I WAS STOPPED FOR THE LIGHT OVER MY LICENSE PLATE, WHICH WAS LIT!!!!"** But I couldn't speak, and I don't understand why.

I sat there listening to David A. Robinson and Audrey Forbush lying back and forth. Audrey Forbush told David the reason I stayed in jail as long as I did was because they forgot about me. She mentioned the name Kevin Krantz. He was supposed to be the reason I was in jail as long as I was. She stated he forgot about me. She also said, "David Robinson, you're not suing him. He takes full responsibility." David said nothing. He sat there as if he were mute.

Eventually, we were separated. The opposing council and insurance agent were led to another room. Then my attorney started pleading for me to settle, telling me that the federal judge in Bay City, Michigan, sent me there to settle. If I did not settle, the federal judge would throw my case out. I would receive nothing. And he had to consider the police side. They had a side too.

At that moment I hollered at him!!! "What are you speaking about???" I asked. "Are you representing the police or me????"

He replied, "I'm just saying they have a side too, and all sides have to be considered."

Judge Morgan walked into the room with a low offer. I told her NO!!!! She told me of a case where someone lost their eye and didn't receive anything. I still told her NO!!!! She walked out. My attorney shared with me that a client from Flint, Michigan, lived in Evergreen Regency Apartment complex located off Lippincott Boulevard that he was representing. This client was paralyzed from a shooting. The case was thrown out of court, and he (David A. Robinson) didn't see that coming!! He started talking about Jose Douglas, sharing with me that Jose knew I was on my way to work. He saw my work badge, and that he didn't want to take me to jail, and he admitted to calling his boss to ask him what to charge me with. I turned and looked at my attorney (David Robinson) and called him a liar!!! I told him Jose Douglas admitted on the witness stand during the preliminary trial he never called his boss. "If you had read the information, you would have known it's on page 25 in the Preliminary Examination taken on November 15, 2006."

At that moment, I couldn't stand Attorney Robinson. He was selling me down the drain. I got up to use the restroom. Upon returning, I heard him and Judge Morgan. He agreed to her offer, telling me to take this offer because he was not coming back to court with me. "Fine," I answered. "I want nothing to do with you either." I took the offer. It was a measly $30,000.

As my mother and I were walking out of the federal court, David Robinson was trying to walk with us. My mother asked what was wrong. I answered, "I understand why it was placed on my heart to write a book. This is a cruel UNjust legal system, and I'm going to expose it."

David heard this. He asked, "You're writing a book?"

"Yes, I am!!!"

"Can I get in on it? I have some things I would like to express in your book."

I didn't answer him. Things were not right with him in that room, and I would figure it out later. I called my pastor. We talked about the settlement, how low it was, and how my attorney (David A. Robinson) abandoned me.

Monday, March 30, 2009, 3:30 p.m. My shift had ended as I walked to the workout center. David A. Robinson was on my mind. I prayed, asking GOD to help me figure things out because I was lost. I started my run on the treadmill. I went over everything that happened March 26th, with the opposing council making a comment that I didn't understand. She spoke of another person that had nothing to do with my case. Later that evening, I called my mother. I asked her, "Did Audrey Forbush tell you how you were dressed better than the officers that just left when you gave your disposition?"

"Yes," she answered.

"THAT'S IT, MOM, the police gave disposition that David hid from me."

She asked me if I was sure. She didn't feel that he would treat me that way. I decided to call tomorrow and make sure.

Tuesday, March 31, 2009. Once I was off work, I sat in my car and called Theophilus Clemons. I greeted him so friendly. I said, "Hey, Theophilus, how you doing??? How's your day???"

He answered all my questions. Now I slipped it in on him. **"HOW MANY OFFICERS GAVE DISPOSITIONS, THEO??"**

He answered four. I asked, "May I get a copy?"

He answered it wasn't up to him. It was up to David. I tried to con him. I said, "David and I are writing a book together." He asked me the name of it. I didn't have a name. I thought of *Nightmare on Outer Dr.* He started laughing, so I slipped it in again. "Can I get those deps?"

He answered, "This is David A. Robinson's law firm. He's the head honcho. I am just a little peon."

I realized I wouldn't get my dispositions. If David wanted me to read them, he would have provided them to me before the settlement hearing. There must be something in there about Timothy Wayne Patterson. I tried to figure out what to do next.

Friday, April 3, 2009, 11:30 A.M. During my break, I called Judge Morgan's chambers and spoke with her secretary, sharing with her David wouldn't give me all the evidence. She told me Judge Morgan couldn't get in the middle of that. I should get in touch with the grievance commission if I felt David had wronged me. I told her yes, he had. She looked up the telephone number and shared it with me. I thanked her.

I made the telephone call. The person I spoke with told me I would receive paperwork in the mail in a few days. Once my paperwork arrived, I wrote out my grievance, telling the commission that David A. Robinson took me to a settlement hearing, concealing evidence from me. I would like a full investigation pertaining to this matter.

By the middle of April I heard from David's office. It's his secretary. She told me my check was there, and I can come and pick it up. I told her no, I'm not coming until I read the dispositions. She said okay, she would speak with Mr. Robinson.

A week later she called back, telling me if I come to the office that I could read all evidence and have the evidence once I signed the release form. I started laughing at her. "Send it in the mail and maybe I'll sign after I've read it. I'm signing nothing until I read all evidence." We ended our phone call. She called back in a couple of days, asking me if I would come in after work and sit in the office and read the material. I told her no again. I asked her, "Do you think I'm going to stand on my legs for 8 hours, and then drive from Flint to Southfield, and have to drive back to Flint? It's 70 minutes each way. You're out of your mind!!!" I said good-bye. I felt bad about being short with her. I really like the lady. She always treated me with great respect, but she was working for a scoundrel. Isn't it amazing how I was so impressed with the name "David," thinking he was a man after GOD'S own heart? Now, I'm calling him a scoundrel. Life is full of lessons. I should have prayed to GOD about David A. Robinson and Theophilus Clemons, instead of believing they were quality men of GOD, sent from GOD.

Tuesday, May 5, 2009. I received a call from David A. Robinson around 5:30 P.M. as I was entering Galaxy Lanes to bowl in the Flint City Tournament. I ignored his call until I was finished. I wished I never looked at my telephone, seeing his number. I bowled extremely badly. I called my voice mail to listen to his message. He made me laugh. He left me his personal cell phone number, instructing me to get in touch with him ASAP!!! "Maybe we can work out something about the disposition." I started to laugh. *There's nothing to be worked out,* I thought to myself. I want the dispositions sent to me in the mail.

Friday, May 8, 2009, I received a letter from David A. Robinson.

Dear Ms. Davis,

On March 26, 2009, we settled your case and the settlement was placed on the record. Therefore, you requested copies of transcripts and file documents to assist you in writing a book about the case.

The release we received, however, contains a "confidentiality clause" which may impact what you wish to write/publish about the case. We have a duty to advise you accordingly. However, you have apparently chosen not to sign the release until you get a copy of the file, and you won't come in to discuss the issues of how the "confidentiality clause" may affect what you put in your book. We are prepared to give you copies of the file. However, we need you to come into the office to get the documents you'd like so we can discharge our corresponding duty to advise you in accordance with the terms of the release. We, therefore, respectfully request that you come in to the office ASAP so we can execute the release and give you the documents you desire in compliance with the confidentiality clause. Then we can disburse your settlement funds and bring this matter to a final close.

David A. Robinson

After reading this, I knew I was right in my judgment regarding David A. Robinson being a "LIAR." I never requested this information to help in writing a book. I wanted to know the truth about Timothy W. Patterson. I still refused to call.

Wednesday, May 13, 2009. I finally receive my paperwork from the grievance commission. I was so excited!!! My excitement, however, quickly deflated. The grievance commission refused to do anything to Attorney Robinson. They informed me if I feel he wrong me, to pursue him in a court of law. At the end of the letter, they stated that they would send David A. Robinson a copy of my complaint against him. I was disappointed in the grievance commission. I really thought they were going to sanction him. I was hurt. I had to go running.

As I ran on the track at Flint Hamady High School, I thought of how I abandoned GOD during my choice of lawyers. I was hung up on names and color of skin. I leaned on my own understanding, but GOD is such a merciful GOD that I was going to pray to him to take over, now that I made a mess of this situation. Only GOD could clean this up. I would put it all in his hands. I concentrated on Proverbs 3:5–6, "Trust in the Lord with all thine heart; and lean not unto thine own understanding. In all thy ways acknowledge him and he shall direct thy path."

Thursday, May 14, 2009, 8:00 A.M. I was up calling lawyers. I was not sure what type of lawyer I needed since the grievance commission didn't share that type of information, so I just made calls. I spoke with a female attorney who shared with me that I was entitled to all evidence before my attorney took me into the settlement hearing. She got on the computer and told me that David A. Robinson was withdrawing as my attorney and petitioning the court to have the settlement enforced. I was shocked!!!! I asked, "Are you sure???"

"Yes," she replied, "I'm looking at it right now. He's taking you back to the federal court in Bay City." She informed me of a few attorneys to get in touch with, and she wished me well in my pursuit of justice. I thanked her for her time. Just as I was making another call, the doorbell rang. I looked out the window and saw the mail truck. I answered the door. It was a certified letter from David A. Robinson. I sat down to read the letter. The attorney was correct. He was withdrawing as my attorney and petitioning the court to enforce the settlement without allowing me to read the dispositions. What kind of justice is this???

Robinson & Associates, P.C. Attorneys and Counselors at Law

David A. Robinson, Esq.
28145 Greenfield Road, Suite 100
Southfield, Michigan 48076-7102
Office: (248) 423-7234, ext. 15
Fax: (248) 423-7227
E-mail: attyclemons@netscape.com

Theophilus E. Clemons, Esq.
R. Mickelle Miller, J.D.
Law Clerk
Sylvia Ross, D.D.S., M.S.
Legal Assistant

May 14, 2009
Regular Mail & Certified Mail Return Receipt Requested
7002 24100 0002 9298 2262
Ms. Kim R. Davis
Re: Kim Davis v City of Buena Vista Police Officer Jose Douglas, Case No. 08-12881-BC, Hon. Thomas L. Ludington

Dear Ms. Davis:
Enclosed please find a copy of Motion to Enforce Settlement and withdraw as Plaintiff's Counsel with Certificate of Service in the above referenced matter.

Sincerely,

Robinson & Associates, P.C.
Theophilus E. Clemons, Attorney & Counselor at law
TEC/SRS
Enclosures: HTTP://WWW.DAVIDROBINSONLAW.COM

The court date was set for Wednesday, June 10, 2009, 3:00 P.M. I prepared myself for this battle with the scoundrels from Southfield, Michigan, by praying and meditating on Hebrews 4:16. "Let us therefore come boldly unto throne of grace, that we may obtain mercy, and find grace to help in time of need." This is one of my pastor George Wilkerson's favorite scriptures. I also prayed that the Lord would grant me favor with Judge Thomas L. Ludington, to touch his heart and softened it toward me, allowing me to receive all evidence.

June 10th arrived. My mother and I drove to Bay City, Michigan. We walked into Judge Ludington's courtroom. I looked to my right. There was the eagle. I immediately thought of Isaiah 40:31, "But they that wait upon the Lord shall renew their strength; they shall mount up with wings as eagles; they shall run, and not be weary; and they shall walk, and not faint."

My mom and I took our seats, and soon, in walked a Caucasian female in her early thirties. She was thin, with blond hair down to the middle of her neck. Very slender. She wore a gray pantsuit. She took a seat up front.

2:57 P.M. In walked Theophilus Clemons wearing a blue suit. He walked immediately up front and caught a glance of me. He walked back to where I was seated, asking me what I was doing there. "Are you trying to get something started in court???"

I told him, "I want evidence."

He told me I was not entitled to all evidence. I showed him a letter that I was given when I was released from Saginaw County Jail, reading that I was entitled to all evidence against me. He informed me that wasn't true. "That's only true in a criminal case, not civil cases."

I called him a "LIAR." I told him I have a right to know everything about the officers involved in my case. "We will see what Judge Ludington has to say about that."

He responded with, "NO, you don't have any rights to all evidence, and you won't speak. This is a federal court. You're not a lawyer. He's not going to allow you to say one word. You wasted your time driving here!!!!!"

I replied, "You don't know what I know and who I know!!!!!" I was speaking of the Father, Son, and Holy Ghost who I prayed to before I came to this courtroom, I thought to myself. My mother asked him, "How come when you're running for office it matters?"

He replied, "That's different." He also said there was explosive evidence on both sides.

I asked, "What was explosive evidence on my side?"

He answered, "You called them names. You said ASSHOLE!!!! AND JACKASS!!!!"

I started laughing. I then asked, "What was explosive on their end?" He became silent. He didn't answer. Now I realized he was a snake just like David Robinson.

Judge Ludington entered the courtroom. Attorney Clemons and the female attorney stood up and both said something about me, but I couldn't make out what they were saying. They both stated their names to Judge Ludington. He looked out directly at me and asked, "Is that Ms. Davis in the pink top?"

Both attorneys looked my way. He informed them he wanted to speak to me. I walked up front with my hand placed in GOD'S unchanging hands, remembering what my pastor, George Wilkerson said, "Stick and stay with Jesus." As I walked, I asked GOD to allow me to speak the truth slowly so the judge would understand all my words. When I get excited I speak too fast.

Once I approached the bench, Attorney Clemons was clearly not happy. I shared with Judge Ludington that evidence was kept from me. I figured it out on the treadmill. He looked over at Attorney Clemons and asked if I did call his office on March 31st to request evidence. Attorney Clemons lied and said I requested evidence from David A. Robinson and not him. "Yes, she did request evidence."

Judge Ludington asked, "Why wasn't it given to Ms. Davis?"

He answered, "Ms. Davis is writing a book about the case. We wanted to inform her of what she could and couldn't write."

Judge Ludington ignored his comments. I was laughing on the inside. He thought that sharing with Judge Ludington my plans to write a book would go against me. It didn't. GOD IS GOOD. Just sit back and let him work. Judge Ludington asked Clemons if I was allowed to read the concise two-page letter they sent to Judge Morgan stating about my case. He answered no. I thought to myself, *That's why David Robinson was happy to go in her courtroom. He never presented my case or wrote to her about my case. What kind of judge is she that only read what Audrey Forbush sent? She should have informed my attorney to send in his paperwork.* I wondered if all three of them were in bed together against me. The judge told him this was backward.

Attorney Clemons asked Judge Ludington to make me pay for his expenses since he drove from Southfield, Michigan, to Bay City, Michigan, which is 102.44 miles. The judge turned and looked at me, asking me where I lived. I told him, and he smiled at me. "You're not that far, are you, Ms. Davis?"

"No sir," I answered, "it's around a 30-minute drive."

He smiled and said, "Good!!" He told Attorney Clemons, "No, you may not have any more money from Ms. Davis!!!" Judge Ludington then asked if he had the dispositions with him.

Attorney Clemons said, "No!!"

Judge Ludington told Attorney Clemons that I had the right to read them. He then asked me if I wanted to go to Attorney David A. Robinson's office to pick up the evidence or have the evidence sent to me. I answered, "I want it sent to me." He then instructed both of us to try to come to a resolution after I read the evidence. If we couldn't, then he told us to return Monday, July 6, 2009, at 2:00 P.M.

As I left the courtroom, Attorney Clemons walked up to me, telling me I would receive all evidence in a harsh voice. He was not a happy camper.

I answered him in the same tone, "That's all I wanted!!!!"

Friday, June 12, 2009. I received the dispositions. The first one I read was Officer Timothy W. Patterson's.

DAVIS v. BUENA VISTA

DEPO TIMOTHY PATTERSON

TAKEN: 1·14-09

UNITED STATES DISTRICT COURT, EASTERN DISTRICT OF MICHIGAN, SOUTHERN DIVISION

KIM R. DAVIS, Plaintiff

CASE NO: 08-12881-BC

vs.

JUDGE LUDINGTON CITY OF BUENA VISTA POLICE OFFICER JOSE DOUGLAS,

CITY OF BUENA VISTA POLICE OFFICER JAIME VILLANUEVA, and

CITY OF BUENA VISTA POLICE OFFICER TIM PATTERSON, Individually and in Their Official Capacities as Police Officers

Defendants

111 East Court Street, Flint, Michigan, commencing at or about 9:38 A.M.

APPEARANCES:

ROBINSON & ASSOCIATES, P.C.
SY:THEOPHILUS E. CLEMONS (P-47991)
28145 Greenfield Road, Suite 100
Southfield, Michigan 48076
(248) 423-7234
Appearing on behalf of the Plaintiff, Ripka, Boroski & Associates
1-800-542-4531/810-234-7785/Fax 810•234-0660
e-mail: rba@ripkaboroskLnet

DAVIS v. BUENA VISTA
DEPO TIMOTHY PATTERSON
TAKEN: 1-14-09
Appearance Continued
Plunkett Conney
By: Audrey J. Forbush (P-41744)

Plaza One Financial Center
111 East Court Street, Suite 1B
Flint, Michigan 48502

Appearing on Behalf of the Defendants
Also Present: Jose Douglas
Witness: Timothy Patterson
Examination by Mr. Clemons
Examination by Ms. Forbush
INDEX OF EXHIBITS
Exhibit 1 (Supplemental Report)
Exhibit 2 (Daily Activity Report)
Exhibit 3 (Drawing) 30
Ripka, Boroski & Associates, 1-800-542-4531/810-234-7785/ Fax 810-234-0660
DAVIS vs. BUENA VISTA DEPO.
TIMOTHY PATTERSON TAKEN: 1-14-09; present, I believe, is Officer Jose Douglas, also present for this deposition.
EXAMINATION

MR. CLEMONS: Is it officer or is there another rank? Officer, could you give us your full name for the record.

Officer Timothy Wayne Patterson.

You are currently employed as an officer with the Buena Vista Police Department?

Yes.

MR. CLEMONS: By the way, if, at any point during this deposition, you would like to change an answer, please let me know, okay?

THE WITNESS: Okay.

MR. CLEMONS: And, also, if at any point you would like to clarify an answer, will you please let me know?

THE WITNESS: Yes.

MR. CLEMONS: At the end of the deposition, if there's an answer you would like to change, would you do so?

We have another person in the room now. Could you identify the party?

MS. FORBUSH: This is the chief of police, Chief Booker.

(Whereupon a brief discussion was held off the record)

MR. CLEMONS: I believe the last question was whether or not—strike that. I'll restate the question. Officer, if at any time you would like to correct an answer, change an answer, add to an answer, at the end of this dep, please let me know so we can have a clear record, okay?

THE WITNESS: Okay.

MR. CLEMONS: Has your rank always been that of officer?

Yes.

How long have you been an officer with the Buena Vista Police Department?

Since July of 2005.

Where did you work before that?

Saginaw Valley State University and Vassar Police Department.

Say that again, please.

Saginaw Valley State University and the Vassar Police.

Now, is that two different jobs?

Yes, it is.

Okay. How did you work or what did you work in law enforcement for Saginaw Valley?

Yes, I did.

What was the nature of the employment?

With the Department of Public Safety, I was a police officer there.

How long did you work as a police officer at Saginaw Valley?

From 1996 to 2002.

Why did you leave?

I was discharged.

For what reason?

MS. FORBUSH: I'll object to relevancy, but you can answer.

THE WITNESS: Conduct unbecoming.

MR. CLEMONS: What conduct was unbecoming that caused you to be discharged from Saginaw Valley law enforcement department?

MS. FORBUSH: And if I can just have a continuing objection, I won't interrupt.

MR. CLEMONS: Yes.

THE WITNESS: Because I jokingly told an officer that I was joking around with regarding another officer from a different agency that I pepper sprayed him, which I did not do.

MR. CLEMONS: Saginaw Valley—you referred to Saginaw Valley, and I want the record to be clear. Are we referring to an educational institution? Saginaw Valley State University?

Yes.

And you were on their public safety force, if you will?

Yes.

And you were terminated because you made a comment that you had pepper sprayed another officer; do I have that correct?

Yes.

And who was the other officer? What was her name, his name?

Jason Hendricks.

And at the time of your discharge—strike that. At the time that you were alleged to have pepper sprayed Officer Hendricks, where was Hendricks employed as a police officer?

Carlton Township Police Department.

Was there an investigation into that incident?

I believe there were interviews; yes.

And you were interviewed?

Yes.

By whom?

Officer Trepkowskl.

Can you spell that, please, if you can.

I believe it's T-R-E-P-K-O-W-S-K-l. He's now the chief of Saginaw Valley State University Public Safety.

And following that interview, the conclusion was that you would be discharged?

Yes.

Now, after leaving Saginaw Valley public safety, you then worked at Carlton, you said?

Vassar.

And what is that?

Police department.

Vassar City?

Yes.

Where is that?

In Vassar, Michigan.

What county?

Tuscola.

What was your period of employment there?

2002 through 2005, when I came to Buena Vista.

And why did you leave Vassar City Police Department?

Because they were going to downsize and terminate my position due to budget constraints, and I was hired at Buena Vista prior to them doing so.

All right, did you leave the Vassar Police Department voluntarily?

Yes.

What's your date of birth, sir?

November 7, 1966.

MR. CLEMONS: For purposes of a potential trial, will you accept any subpoena that—

MS. FORBUSH: Absolutely.

MR. CLEMONS: You began with the Buena Vista Police Department in 2005, correct? July 2005, right?

Correct.

When you applied to work at the Vassar City Police Department, did you inform any person by way of document application or verbally as to your discharge from Saginaw Valley and the reason therefore?

MS. FORBUSH: Object to relevancy. You can answer.

THE WITNESS: Yes.

MR. CLEMONS: How did you inform any person at Saginaw Valley—at Vassar that you had been discharged from Saginaw Valley?

MS. FORBUSH: Same objection.

THE WITNESS: I believe it was on the application.

MR. CLEMONS: And to your recollection, what did you put on the application with respect to your employment at Saginaw Valley?

MS. FORBUSH: If I could have a continuing objection.

MR. CLEMONS: Continuing objection noted.

THE WITNESS: If I'm not mistaken, the application asks why you leave, and I said discharged.

MR. CLEMONS: Prior to working at Saginaw Valley, where did you work?

The Saginaw County Juvenile Detention Center.

In what capacity, sir?

I was a Detention Youth Care Specialist for a short time, and then I became a Detention Supervisor.

And that was for what period, from beginning to end?

1989 until I was hired at Saginaw Valley.

And what were the circumstances of leaving that particular job?

To become a police officer.

You left voluntarily?

Yes.

Where did you work prior to that?

I was in college, and I had several part-time jobs.

Any of those part-time jobs in law enforcement or with relation to the enforcement of any laws?

No.

Now, the job you referred to a moment ago, in the detention center, I believe, you said . . .

Yes.

During the course of your employment there, were you ever subjected to any discipline?

MS. FORBUSH: Object to relevancy, but you can answer.

THE WITNESS: I don't recall if I've been written up. I never had any days off. 1 don't remember if I've ever been written up for any policy violation.

MR. CLEMONS: Do you recall receiving any type of discipline of any description while working in your capacity as an employee at the detention center, if you will?

MS. FORBUSH: Same objection.

THE WITNESS: I don't recall off the top of my head.

MR. CLEMONS: With respect to your employment as a Saginaw Valley public safety officer, did you ever receive any discipline?

MS. FORBUSH: Same objection.

THE WITNESS: I may have, but I don't know exactly what it was off the top of my head other than the discharge.

MR. CLEMONS: Okay. So with respect to Saginaw Valley, other than the discharge, you can't say for certain that you were not disciplined otherwise?

No, I cannot.

Do you believe you received any complaints from any of the students or other persons on the campus with respect to your conduct?

In respect to my conduct, yes sir. Citizen complaints.

MS. FORBUSH: Same objection.

THE WITNESS: I'm sure there were. I don't remember any specifics.

MR. CLEMONS: With respect to your employment at Vassar City, were you the subject of any citizen complaints?

MS. FORBUSH: Object to relevance.

THE WITNESS: Again, I'm sure I was.

MR. CLEMONS: What was the outcome of any of those complaints?

MS. FORBUSH: Continuing objection as to relevance.

THE WITNESS: Unfounded.

MR. CLEMONS: Do you have any idea how many?

No, I don't.

Do you know what they pertain to with respect to the citizens' complaints?

Not specifics, no.

Did they deal with an abuse of authority?

MS. FORBUSH: Object to relevancy.

THE WITNESS: No.

MR. CLEMONS: Do you have any reasonable number as to how many citizen complaints there were while at Vassar City?

Again, I don't recall.

Were you ever the subject of any Internal Affairs Investigation?

MS. FORBUSH: Object to relevancy. You can answer.

THE WITNESS: Yes.

MR. CLEMONS: How many?

One that I'm aware of.

MS. FORBUSH: If I could just have a continuing objection as to relevancy, please.

MR. CLEMONS: Yes. Tell me the circumstances of the Internal Affairs Investigation.

We had a scheduled firearms training on a Saturday morning. I went out the night before and had a few drinks. Apparently, when I got to work that day for the firearms training, they could still smell alcohol on my person, not from my breath; and that was the basis of it.

I see, was there—strike that. What was the conclusion of the investigation?

Letter in my file.

Stating what?

I don't have the letter in front of me. I can't tell you verbatim what it said.

Were you disciplined in the letter?

I believe it was a written verbal warning.

Is it correct to say that as a result of the Vassar Internal Affairs Investigation, you received a written form of discipline which included that you had come to a firearms training session while allegedly intoxicated?

No.

MS. FORBUSH: I'm going to object to the form of the question and to foundation.

MR. CLEMONS: Absolutely I can clarify. I don't understand, sir; you received a letter of discipline for what?

Because I went out drinking the night before a training session.

And the training session was to begin at what time? In the morning, right?

It was sometime in the morning. I can't remember if it was 8 or 9 o'clock.

And when you arrived, it was the allegation that there was alcohol on your breath?

No, sir; I did not say that. I said on my person. I did not shower after I got up that morning.

I see. Who was the author of the letter?

I believe it was written by Chief Dave Meniere.

All right. And what was the event that you had arrived at having not showered?

A firearms training that was outside.

And aside from that incident, any other Internal Affairs Investigations?

Not to my knowledge.

Have you ever entered a plea in any court with respect to any criminal charge?

No.

Have you ever been convicted of any criminal charge?

No.

Have you ever been involved in any prior lawsuits?

Yes.

How many?

One.

MS. FORBUSH: If I could just have a continuing objection as to relevancy, please.

MR. CLEMONS: Noted. You were involved in one prior civil lawsuit separate and apart from this one?

Yes.

In what court?

I'm not sure what court it was in.

Is it ongoing as we speak?

No.

When did it end, to your knowledge?

Honestly, I can't tell you because it was ongoing when I was at Saginaw Valley State University, and I was discharged prior to the conclusion or settlement.

I see. What was the conclusion of the lawsuit?

I don't truly know.

You were a named defendant?

I was one of several, yes.

And what was the allegation?

Excessive use of force.

And who was the plaintiff?

I can't remember his first name, but his last, I believe, was Lapann.

And to your recollection, where did the alleged excessive use of force take place, what city?

On the campus of Saginaw Valley State University.

Was there an investigation of that by any investigative body or person at Saginaw Valley, as far as an Internal Affairs Investigation? As far as any type of investigation?

Not to my knowledge.

Did that involve the use of a weapon?

No. Correct that. Pepper spray was used but not by myself.

No firearms?

No.

Officer, did you author, write any documents pertaining to a stop of Kim R. Davis in September of 2006?

Yes, I did.

Please tell me all of the documents that you authored.

It was a supplemental to Officer Douglas's report.

Anything else?

No.

Did you give verbal information to any superior officer pertaining to the incident?

Unless they were on scene, no.

Was there any investigation of the incident by any other officer higher in rank than you?

Not to my knowledge.

The supplemental document you referred to, did you review it before this deposition?

Yes, I did.

Do you have it with you, sir?

Yes, I do.

In the Notice of Deposition, it's a duces tecum request, meaning that you are to bring all documents pertaining to it. Have you done that, sir?

Documents I prepared, yes.

Are you aware of any other documents other than which you prepared pertaining to the incident?

There are other reports and supplemental reports, yes, but I did not bring them because I did not produce them.

That's right. Okay. Are there any other documents that you're aware of that contain any statements by yourself?

Not that I'm aware of.

Were you working that evening, September 29th of '06, by yourself, in a car by yourself?

Yes.

The supplemental document that you referenced, when did you generate that document?

When did I originally type the report?

Did you type a report?

Yes.

Arid you typed it into a computer?

Yes.

When did you originally type the report?

The day that the incident occurred.

Would that have been at the end of your shift?

It may have been during.

Is it correct that you don't have a recollection as to whether you generated your supplemental report either during your shift or at the end of your shift; is that correct?

I write my reports when I get an opportunity. It could have been during. It could have been at the end.

Okay. However, whether at the end or during, was it close in time to the actual event? It wasn't the next day?

No (I would assume it happened right then and there that day).

Okay. What is it—is there a technical name for the document you completed?

It's a supplemental report to Officer Douglas's report. To get to my location, if he got that far.

Okay. And you went and sat at what street?

It's a triangle intersection. It's Kinney Road and North Street comes together at Outer Drive.

As best you can, can you show me? And if you could, sir, put the location where you were sitting, the street which the other two vehicles were coming toward you on.

MS. FORBUSH: I don't know if this will help, but I printed a little map. (Whereupon Deposition Exhibit 3 was marked for identification by the court reporter)

No.

There's no rain or anything like that? Clear night?

I believe it was.

Okay. What was the speed of the vehicle of Ms. Davis? Okay, recognizing that this is out of scale, what is the rectangle with the number two in it? What does that represent?

Officer Douglas's vehicle.

And then the rectangle with what looks like S-U-S-P, that's the vehicle which would be Kim Rose Davis?

Yes.

Can you put an arrow on there, please, that shows me which direction—show me which way they are coming, sir.

(Witness complies.)

Now, the street they're on, that's Outer Drive?

Yes, it is.

Point where they passed you—and they did pass you, correct?

Yes.

At the point where they passed you, was there a hazard lane?

You mean a shoulder?

Yes, sir.

Very, very small shoulder due to the large ditch. On the east side of the road, there's a guardrail.

Okay. Is Outer Drive, at that point, a two-lane, four-lane? How many lanes?

It's two lanes.

And if you could specify, is that one headed north and one headed south? I see. When they passed you at your location and your location is what you have marked as the number one, sir?

Yes.

Your vehicle is facing south, is that correct?

Yes.

And you're observing both Ms. Rose Davis's car and that of Officer Douglas?

Yes.

You have a clear unobstructed view?

I didn't have radar on. I couldn't tell you.

You had radar, though, didn't you?

No, I did not. Correct that. Yes, I did on my dally. I had a Talon handheld, but I didn't have it in my hand at that time.

Did you perceive her to be speeding?

I would say she was going as fast as the normal flow of traffic through there.

Did you observe her in the proper lane as she approached you?

Yes.

Did she appear to be swerving or unable to maintain control of her vehicle?

I truthfully didn't pay that close attention to that part.

I believe you said that the lights of Officer Douglas's vehicle were on?

Yes.

Do you know what the approximate distance was between the two vehicles? Could you tell that?

I don't recall.

MS. FORBUSH: Just for clarification, we're talking about emergency lights, overheads?

MR. CLEMONS: I'll clarify; yes. When you observed the vehicles, Officer Patterson, were the emergency lights of Officer Douglas on?

Yes.

What about a siren?

Yes.

Did you see any other vehicles?

No.

Is the intersection that you were at a controlled intersection?

It is from North and Kinney. There are stop signs at those locations.

Other than the stop signs, are there any electronic devices to control the intersection?

No.

What would this be here? What are these? Train tracks?

Train tracks.

So you were sitting approximately, what, half a block from train tracks?

Yes.

So your recollection is Sergeant Baker and Officer Villanueva left before you, Officer Douglas, and Kim Rose Davis left the scene?

Yes.

Turning back to when you first approached the vehicle of Ms. Davis, you indicated that you heard a statement made by Officer Douglas to her; is that correct?

Yes.

And what was the statement again, sir?

He was instructing her to get out of the vehicle.

All right. Did you ever observe any mechanical defects on the vehicle of Ms. Rose Davis?

No.

Did you search her vehicle?

I don't believe I did.

Who instructed her to get out of the vehicle?

Officer Douglas did.

And did she do so?

Eventually, yes.

Now, when you say eventually, how much time elapsed between when he asked her or directed her to get out of the vehicle and when she actually exited the vehicle?

I didn't time it, but he requested her several times; more than two, as many as four.

Villanueva, correct?

You mean Ms. Davis?

I keep saying that. Old. You perform a pat down of any description of Ms. Davis before Officer Villanueva arrived?

No, I did not.

Did Officer Douglas do that?

I don't believe so.

Why didn't you do that?

Because we had a female officer available that could do that.

Is there any policy or procedure that precludes you from performing a pat down, an external pat down of a female?

No, there's not a policy that prevents that.

Have you ever done that prior to this instance? Have you ever patted down a female following a stop?

Yes.

Was there a particular reason why you didn't do so in this case?

Because of her mannerisms and how she was acting.

Wouldn't that suggest all the more reason to pat her down?

She was handcuffed. After she was handcuffed, there was no need to pat her down when a female officer was available.

I see. So Officer Villanueva pats her down, and the pat down is occurring while she's handcuffed, correct?

Correct.

The pat down is a Terry pat down, correct?

Yes.

Police, Lawyers & Judges

There's never an invasive more—more invasive pat down or search of Ms. Davis that evening to your knowledge, is that correct?

Not in my presence.

You were not concerned for your safety prior to the arrival of Officer Villanueva, were you?

There was an issue as far as how Ms. Davis was acting. I was in fear for my safety as far as her actually assaulting me.

Now let me ask you. You indicated that, based on your experience, her mannerisms suggested that she might have been intoxicated, correct?

Yes.

The mannerisms that you described, are they consistent with someone who may have been under the influence of drugs?

Yes.

Were you concerned that there may have been drugs on her person?

It's a possibility, but I don't remember being concerned by it.

So the idea of patting her down for, perhaps, drugs or some other illegal substance, that wasn't a concern either?

Again, once she was handcuffed, we waited for Officer Villanueva, because if she's a female officer, she can search her.

I'm talking about prior to handcuffing her.

I did not.

And my question was: Prior to her being handcuffed, given her mannerisms that gave you concern, it didn't cross your mind to search her for, perhaps, drugs or something like that?

I wasn't threatened by what drugs she might have in her pockets.

Understandably. But drugs are illegal, correct?

Yes, they are.

And so, again, my question is: Did it cross your mind to search her for drugs?

MS. FORBUSH: Objection to relevancy, form. You can answer if you can.

THE WITNESS: Again, I did not fear for any drugs jumping out of her pockets or being assaulted by any drugs she may have in her pocket. We had a female officer available to do a search of her like I told you prior, so that's what occurred.

MR. CLEMONS: All right, you would agree that while her hands were free, if she had any drugs, she could have attempted to discard them; would you agree?

Yes.

Once Officer Villanueva completed her pat down, what happened next?

Ms. Davis was placed back in the vehicle, Officer Douglas's vehicle, in the same seat that she had exited from.

And then where did you go?

Shortly thereafter, I believe, I asked Officer Douglas if he needed me to do anything. And he had already contacted a wrecker, which is Gobeyn's, our wrecker service that we use, to come and impound Ms. Davis's vehicle. I went back to my patrol vehicle until Gobeyn's arrived and removed the vehicle, at which time Officer Douglas transported Ms. Davis to the Saginaw County Jail.

Can you describe or show me, as we sit here, how you put your hand on Ms. Davis during the course of the search by Officer Villanueva?

DAVIS v. BUENA VISTA DEPO
JOSE DOUGLAS
TAKEN: 1-14-09
UNITED STATES DISTRICT COURT, EASTERN DISTRICT OF MICHIGAN, SOUTHERN DIVISION
KIM R. DAVIS, Plaintiff,
CASE NO: 08-12881-BC
vs.
JUDGE LUDINGTON CITY OF BUENA VISTA POLICE OFFICER JOSE DOUGLAS,
CITY OF BUENA VISTA POLICE OFFICER JAIME VILLANUEVA, and
CITY OF BUENA VISTA POLICE OFFICER TIM PATTERSON, Individually and in Their Official Capacities as Police Officers.
Defendants

The Deposition of JOSE DOUGLAS, taken on Wednesday, January 14, 2009, at 111 East Court Street, Flint, Michigan, commencing at or about 11:40 A.M.

APPEARANCES:

ROBINSON & ASSOCIATES, P.C.
BY: THEOPHILUS E. CLEMONS (P-47991)
28145 Greenfield Road, Suite 100
Southfield, Michigan 48076
(248) 423-7234

Appearing on behalf of the Plaintiff,
Flint, Michigan, Wednesday, January 14, 2009
JOSE DOUGLAS

A witness herein, having been duly sworn, I was examined and testified under oath as follows:

MR. CLEMONS: The record should reflect that this is the time and place for the deposition of Officer Jose Douglas being taken pursuant to Notice to be used for all allowable purposes under the Federal Rules of Evidence, Federal Rules of Civil Procedure.

Officer Douglas, my name is Theophilus Clemons, and along with David Robinson, we represent Kim Rose Davis in a matter before the Honorable Thomas Ludington, U.S. District Court.

EXAMINATION BY MR. CLEMONS:

Have you ever had your deposition taken before?
No, sir.
You were present for the deposition of Officer Patterson, correct?
Yes, sir.
You heard the instructions given?
Yes, sir.
And you heard the questions I asked Officer Patterson?
Yes.
And you heard his responses, correct?
Yes, sir.

Before I begin with specific questions, are there any answers that you heard him give that stuck out in your mind as being contrary to what transpired?

No, sir, not that I can recall at this time.

MR. CLEMONS: Now, just briefly, please don't answer any questions until I finish my question. And, also, if your counsel has an objection, please don't answer. Interestingly, you had very few objections in the last dep. That was amazing. You must want to get out of here.

MS. FORBUSH: You're asking good questions.

MR. CLEMONS: Officer, if I ask a question, we'll presume you understood it and answered it truthfully, okay?

THE WITNESS: Yes, sir.

MR. CLEMONS: And if there's any question that's not clear, please tell me so I can make it clearer, all right?

THE WITNESS: Yes, sir. Yes, sir.

When you saw his vehicle, did you maintain radio contact with Officer Patterson? With anyone?

I just kept updating Central Dispatch what was going on, that I'm continuing on and that's it and the direction that we were heading.

Okay. During the entire interaction with her, did she ever attempt to physically harm you?

She hit my hand.

Other than that?

Other than that, not that I can remember.

In your report, it indicates that she said to you, quote, "I will whoop your ass."

Yes, sir. She did make threats.

Now, I see the one threat, "I will whoop your ass." Were there other similar threats made to you by her?

Yes, sir.

What were they?

She told me that if she sees me out somewhere, she was going to whoop my ass.

When did she say that to you?

She said that when I was en route to the Saginaw County Jail with her.

Okay. Any other threats?

No, sir, not that I can recall.

So if I understand you correctly, there was a threat made, "I will whoop your ass," while you were on the scene; and then there was a second threat made in the vehicle en route to the Saginaw County Jail?

Yes, sir.

And to the best of your recollection, those were the only two verbal threats made by her to you?

She did a lot of other curses, but I can't remember everything else she said.

I'm only asking you about threats.

Yes, sir.

Did you hear her making threats toward Officer Patterson?

Not that I can recall, sir.

Did you hear her make any threats to Officer Villanueva?

No, sir, not that I can recall.

Did you hear her make any threats to Sergeant Baker?

I didn't hear her make any threats toward Sergeant Baker. I wasn't there.

How much do you weigh now, sir?

About 240 maybe, 250.

Were you approximately that size at the time of this stop?

Yes, sir. I was about the same size.

And your height, sir?

I'm five eleven and a half.

According to your report, Ms. Davis was engaged in a blank stare?

Yes, sir.

And that was when you first approached the vehicle?

Yes, sir.

Did that give you concern?

It gave me a little concern, but I saw her hands on the steering wheel.

Her hands were at the 10 o'clock and 2 o'clock position?

Yes, sir.

So her hands were on the 10 o'clock and 2 o'clock position on the steering wheel and she was engaged in a blank stare straight-ahead when you approached the vehicle?

Yes, sir.

That gave you concern? And my only question is: As she did that, did you perceive in your mind she's trying to strike you?

I really can't say that she was; if she was really trying to harm me, she would have done that.

So what happened at that point?

We were on the side of the road. I asked her a couple of questions. And then I told her to go back to the vehicle.

Let me stop you there. What questions did you ask her?

I asked her had she been drinking.

Anything else?

I asked her was she on any type of medication, drugs, or anything.

Okay. Please continue, if there's anything else.

No. Those are the only two questions I can recall asking.

Did she respond to those questions?

She said she hadn't been drinking, and I can't even remember the response to the drugs.

Now, you had a concern for drugs. Did you have a concern to pat her down for drugs?

No, sir, I didn't. I didn't have a concern to pat her down.

So you asked her, you directed her, to the rear of the vehicle?

Yes, sir.

UNITED STATES DISTRICT COURT

EASTERN DISTRICT OF MICHIGAN, SOUTHERN DIVISION

KIM R. DAVIS,

Plaintiff,

-vs.-

CITY OF BUENA VISTA P.O. JOSE DOUGLAS, P.O. JAIME VILLANUEVA and P.O. TIM PATTERSON, Individually and in their official capacities as police officers.

Defendants
Case #08-12881 BC
The deposition of P.O. JAIME VILLANUEVA
Acting in the county of Genesee, at 111 East Court Street, in the city of Flint, State of Michigan, on January 19, 2009, commencing at or about the hour of 10:00 o'clock A.M. APPEARANCES:

THEOPHILUS E. CLEMONS, ESQUIRE
David A. Robinson & Associates
28145 Greenfield Road, suite 100
Southfield, Michigan 48076
248-423-7234
Appearing on behalf of the Plaintiff
RELIANCE COURT REPORTING
313-964-3611

Defendants.
Yes.
North and south of Fuller?
Yes.
Was her vehicle in front of one of these construction company buildings?
Yes. You could say, in front of them.
Yes. As in, like her vehicle was here and the buildings were all—all going down the east side. Were those buildings well lit?
Yes.
Did you see any interaction, physical interaction between Douglas and Ms. Davis?
No.
Did you ever see Officer Douglas touch her?
No.
Did you see Officer Patterson touch Ms. Davis?
Yes.
Describe what you saw.
Officer Patterson touched Ms. Davis while I was searching Ms. Davis.

And can you describe the manner in which he touched Ms. Davis? Strike that. Can you describe the manner in which Officer Patterson touched Ms. Davis?

He took one of his hands and placed it between her shoulder blades so that she couldn't turn around on me.

Which hand did he use?

I'm not sure which hand.

What was he doing with his other hand that was not in her back?

I'm not sure what he was doing with his other hand.

Did he ever have his hands on her arm?

Not that I—I couldn't recall.

Did Ms. Douglas ever—Did Ms. Davis ever physically threaten you?

Yes. Okay. Actually, I guess, I would not take it as a threat. She swore at me.

Yes. And that would be verbal, correct?

Yes.

Did she ever take any physical action? Strike that. Did Ms. Davis ever make any furtive gestures that you observed?

By furtive—what do you mean by "furtive"?

Strike that. Did Ms. Davis ever make any physical motions toward you that you perceived as a physical threat?

Yes.

What was that?

That would be as she turned around on me twice as I was searching her.

Initially, her back was to you?

Yes.

What did she do as you—that you perceived as a physical threat?

While I was searching her I was bent down. I was searching her legs and neck; my head was down toward her waist. She turned around on me.

Obviously, when you are searching somebody, you don't know what they are doing. That's a little threat to you when they turn around on you and kind of jump toward you when your head is down that far.

Is it your testimony that she jumped toward you?

No. When she turned around, my head was toward her waist, so, obviously, my face is a few inches from her waist. That's when I jumped back up. That's when I—her turning around on me, I take that as a threat when I'm searching somebody.

All right. Where were your hands on her when she turned around toward you?

My hands were—I was searching her pockets toward her jacket.

When she turned around on you, your hands were in her jacket pocket?

No. I was patting down her jacket pockets.

You were patting down the outer portion of—or of her jacket pockets when she turned around on you?

Yes.

When she turned around on you, were her hands down?

Yes.

What were you searching her for?

For weapons or contraband, anything at all.

When you say, contraband, does that include drugs?

Yes.

Does—You were searching—Were you searching her for drugs?

Yes.

Were you searching her for weapons?

Yes.

Were you searching her for other contraband?

Yes.

Did you find any of those things other than the dog spray?

No.

The only thing you found was dog spray, correct?

Yes.

Did your search go beyond just an outer pat down?

Yes.

Where else did you search her then?

I searched the outer pocket of her jeans and whatever pants she had on, obviously; her sweatshirt and everything.

Was that the extent of her search?

Yes.

Was she ever required to expose any parts of her skin . . .
No.
. . . to you?
No.
Did you ever—did you ever touch her breasts?
No.
Did you ever touch her buttock to go into her pocket? I mean, if that is what you consider touching her buttocks—other than that?
No.
Okay. Did you ever touch in her genital area?

Just as I thought, he's dirty. I couldn't believe how Attorney Theophilus Clemons threw me under the bus and sold me down the drain. He allowed three officers in the room together, Timothy W. Patterson, Jose Douglas, and Chief Brian Booker, when there is only supposed to be one person. How in the world was that fair to me?

As I finished reading the dispositions of Timothy W. Patterson, I thought to myself, what kind of civil rights lawyers are Theophilus Clemons and David A. Robinson??? Attorney Clemons encouraged the police to defame my character. He allowed Timothy W. Patterson to call me a drunk. He let that man say that I was intoxicated. Theophilus Clemons tried to encourage them to say I was trying to throw drugs away.

After reading the dispositions I called Attorney Clemons on the phone. He wasn't in. I left him a voice mail screaming in the phone, **"HOW DARE YOU DEFAME MY CHARACTER AND EQUATE ME WITH DRUGS AND ALCOHOL??!! LET ME TELL YOU SOMETHING. YOU BETTER KEEP YOUR BIG UGLY SELF AWAY FROM ME. DO NOT APPROACH ME IN THAT COURTROOM, AND I MEAN THAT. I DON'T WANT TO SEE YOU OR DAVID. I HAVE NEVER DRUNK ALCOHOLIC BEVERAGES OR USED DRUGS!!!!!!!!"**

Once I hung up the telephone, I had to reach for my Bible. I was ready to fight David and Theophilus. As upset as I was, I could fight both of them at the same time, but I decided to read the Bible instead. When I turned my Bible to Isaiah 54:17, I read, "No weapon that is formed against thee shall prosper; and every tongue that shall rise against thee in judgment thou shalt condemn. This is the heritage of the servants of the LORD, and their righteousness is of me, saith the LORD."

After reading the dispositions and reading how my lawyer threw me under the bus, I found it heartbreaking that this man presented himself to me as a civil rights attorney. He treated me as if I was a nightmare instead of the "dream" he called me when I first went to his office on February 14, 2008. It hurt that an African-American civil rights attorney would treat me in this manner, but I must remember I turned my back on GOD, believing in David Robinson. I was hung up on names instead of my faith in GOD. I couldn't wait to get back to the federal court in Bay City, Michigan, to tell Judge Ludington the information that Robinson and Associates hid from me.

July 6, 2009, 2:00 P.M. As I sat in my car I noticed a Caucasian female walking up the steps of the courthouse in a black suit, white blouse, and black shoes with the color coming off her right heel. I wondered who she was.

The time was near for me to enter the courtroom. Once inside of courthouse I saw five lawyers, three Caucasian males and two Caucasian females. The women were talking. I glanced over at them. One was the female that was against me, and she represented the police. I didn't understand why she was here. I thought this was between Robinson Associates and me. She had on a blue pantsuit. When they noticed me they all became silent. We just stared at each other as adversaries.

I entered the courtroom and took my seat. A minute passed, and here came the woman in the black suit with the paint missing off the heel of her left shoe, asking me to sign papers. I asked, "Who are you?" She informed me she works for David Robinson and that I could go ahead and sign papers and get this over with. I said, "Are you crazy?? I am not signing anything!!!" She stared at me for a moment. Then I turned my back on her, and she kept on speaking, telling me she heard the message I left for Attorney Clemons and would I like to talk about it with her. I answered her, "I don't like those people you work for and please get out of my face." Finally, she got the hint and walked up front.

Once Judge Ludington entered, he spoke to everyone, and he called my name. "Hi, Ms. Davis!!! How are you???"

"Fine," I answered, "how are you, Judge?"

"Good, Ms. Davis!!!" Then he asked, "Are you happy, Ms. Davis, with the information that you wanted?"

I replied, "No sir!"

He told me to come and tell him why. I informed him how David A. Robinson lied to me. "He promised me that he would check out Officer Timothy W. Patterson's information when we were here on the 17th of February. When I asked him on March 26 if he had done so, he said he 'dropped the ball; he forgot to run the information.' However, the paperwork that I have here states the dispositions of the police were taken a week after mine, which was the 14th of January 2009. That man lied to me!!!" I explained to the judge, "Timothy Patterson's record shows that he was fired from Saginaw Valley State University from conduct unbecoming of a police officer. He has complaints from everywhere he worked. This man is a menace to society. Timothy W. Patterson stated that he has complaints against him from every police department he's worked at. He's also been involved in a prior lawsuit against him. He himself stated at a firearm training session that he was scheduled for that he went out the night before, had a few drinks, and when he got to the firearm training they could smell alcohol on him, that it wasn't from his breath. It was reeking out of his pores because he's nasty and didn't take a shower before his firearm training."

At that moment, I was interrupted by Attorney Racine Miller who was representing David A. Robinson. She interrupted, telling the judge I was informed when the dispositions of the police were being taken. I turned and looked her dead in her eyes and told her she was a liar!!! I said, "I would have taken off work and been there; plus, I don't know you, so how can you stand there and say what I was told!!!" The judge stopped us, which was a good thing. I was ready to pop her upside her head!!!

Judge Ludington asked me when I met Theophilus Clemons. I replied, "The day I gave my dispositions, which was January 7th."

He asked Attorney Racine Miller where David A. Robinson was. She replied, "He was out of town with his family for 4th of July holiday." I almost started laughing. I know she was lying. He didn't want to face me because I found out what a skunk he is!!!

The judge started speaking to both attorneys. I took my seat once he finished speaking. He sided with me. He explained to me that he had to enforce the settlement, but he wouldn't force me to sign the confidentiality clause. When he said that, both attorneys jumped up, stating that I had to sign that clause!!!!! How could he award me money without signing for it? He explained to them, "Ms. Davis is not happy with the way she was treated by her attorney, so she's not going to sign anything. I will sign and enforce the settlement." Both attorneys stormed out.

As I began to exit the courtroom, Judge Ludington stopped me and said, "Ms. Davis, pursue him in another courtroom, do you hear me???"

"Yes," I replied.

"Pursue him, I mean it!!!!" Judge Ludington stated.

I smiled and told him, "Good-bye and thank you for being fair." He smiled back.

I shared with my mother how GOD answered prayers. "David A. Robinson, Audrey Forbush, and Chief Brian Booker thought they were the big three and could hide evidence and think they could treat me as if I'm ignorant, but the Father, Son, and Holy Ghost are the only big three, and when it's my time, my big three will mount me on wings of eagles. I will run and not get faint. I will pray and not walk, and GOD is my all in all. I will never let go of his unchanging hand."

My mother said, "Amen."

As I opened the door to exit the courtroom, to my right there stood the two female Caucasian lawyers holding a conversation. I stopped for a moment. They were staring at me, so I stared back. They were looking at me, as if . . . how could this twelfth-grade high school graduate beat us in the courtroom? I smiled and turned to my left to exit the courthouse. I thought about the late Pastor Emeritus Brady who taught me that I have a voice. He taught me to look people in their eyes, to stand as if I am somebody because I belong to the Father, Son, and Holy Ghost, and to never let go of **GOD'S** unchanging hand. What a friend I have in Jesus. I thought of my childhood, of how I was afraid to speak, but this grown woman had something to say now. The late Pastor Brady taught me as long as I was telling the truth, **GOD** will edify my words. I drove back home a happy camper.

July 10, 2009, my telephone was ringing off the hook; so was my cell phone. It was someone from David A. Robinson's office. I didn't take the calls. I was trying to find me a lawyer who specialized in malpractice suits. I finally heard of one who was located in Livonia, Michigan. I made an appointment to speak with Attorney Riley P. Richards. I interpreted his name to be mean *rough* and *ready*. He came highly recommended, but, of course, I was taking it to the Lord first. Once I met with him he explained to me he's expensive and that when he goes to court he takes experts with him, and they must be paid up front. I asked him his price. He answered $15,000. I almost fell off the chair. I sat there in silence. I said to him, "I will think about it. I had in my mind $5,000, so I would have to pray and think this over." We shook hands and said our good-byes.

July 15, 2009, 10:43 A.M. I received a call from David A. Robinson (my voice mail) stating, "I want you to call either the office or my cell phone number to discuss your options, your rights/resolution concerning drastic steps to resolve your claim, or we can discuss this matter in front of the Michigan State Bar ethics committee to get this matter resolved. Looking forward to speaking with you. Have a nice day, David Robinson." **I WAS NOT CALLING THAT SKUNK!!!!** He had the check; he could take his portion out and send me mine. I would not set foot in that snake pit in Southfield, Michigan. I felt if I went to his office, he would have a document underneath whatever I was supposed to sign and trick me into signing the confidentiality clause, so I would not deal with David A. Robinson.

As the summer progressed, I continued with my running and praying, asking GOD if I should follow through with Judge Ludington's orders to pursue this man in a malpractice suit. The price tag had me going in circles.

Saturday, August 15, 2009. I tried to cancel my subscription with the *Detroit News*. I couldn't, the operator I spoke with told me. "Sunday through Friday is when you can cancel." I found that to be odd, but I wrote myself a note to call and cancel when I came home from church. Instead, that Sunday, I went to Detroit to church with my friend. I arrived home late. The office was closed for whatever reason, so I threw the note away.

Police, Lawyers & Judges

Thursday, August 20, 2009. As I opened the door, there's the paper. I thought to myself, *I am going to cancel when I return home from my run.* Once I returned from my run, I showered, drank a cup of green tea, ate my oatmeal, then I decided to read the paper. To my surprise, I noticed on the front page an article stating Royal Oak settlement averts trial. The city of Royal Oak agreed to a six-figure settlement in a wrongful arrest case involving two Windsor men, ages 35 and 28, who said they were wrongly arrested and jailed after two officers falsely accused them of assault outside DTE Energy Music Theatre in 2003. Two other men pleaded guilty to the crime. I had to turn to Metro 4A for the rest of the story. To my surprise, there's a picture of the two men and their lawyers—*David A. Robinson and Racine Miller.* Now I felt the reason why he threw me under the bus was that he devalued my case because I was an African-American female. He'd rather have his picture in the paper with Caucasian males.

After reading the whole article, I noticed David A. Robinson's statement saying the trial before the jury revealed a "**WEB OF DECEIT BY THE POLICE.**" How dare he make that statement when *he's* the master of deceit! This man withheld evidence from me. This man lied to me, telling me police get immunity. I was on fire. I had to go back to Flint Hamady High School to walk this off. I wanted David A. Robinson so bad I could taste him!! Nowhere in the contract I signed was a statement that he could withhold evidence from me.

Tuesday, September 1, 2009. I made an appointment with lawyer Riley P. Richards from Livonia, Michigan. As soon as I sat down I handed him the money, and I told him I wanted David A. Robinson. My new attorney told me he knew I would be back. He said I had a look of determination. I told him, "Let's do it!!!" I showed him the article in the paper. I told him I felt that Attorney Robinson used me to get those men their settlement. After going over some paperwork, we shook hands, and I told him, "I want your best. You have to bring down this scoundrel from Southfield, Michigan."

September 19, 2009. A big Caucasian male started banging on my door. I didn't answer. I didn't know him, but he wouldn't go away, so I grabbed my knife, put my hand behind my back, and opened the door, and I said, "What do you want??"

He told me he's a process server. He had paperwork for me. I accepted, and he said, "I bet you can't guess who it's from."

David A. Robinson was suing me for breach of contract. He had 18 counts against me. They're laughable. He was suing me in the 67th District Court in Flushing, Michigan.

STATE OF MICHIGAN
IN THE 67TH DISTRICT COURT, FLUSHING, MICHIGAN
ROBINSON & ASSOCIATES, P.C.
A Michigan Professional Corporation
Case No. GCA09-1347
Plaintiff,
Hon.
Kim R. Davis
Defendant,

Robinson and Associates, P.C.
David A. Robinson (P 38754)
Theophilus E. Clemons (P 47991)
Attorneys for Plaintiff
28145 Greenfield Road
Suite 100
Southfield, Michigan 48076
(248) 423-7234

PLAINTIFF'S COMPLAINT

No civil action between these same parties arising out of the transaction or occurrence alleged in the Complaint has been previously filed and/or dismissed in this court, nor is such action pending.

David A. Robinson (P 38754)

NOW COMES Plaintiff, Robinson & Associates, P.C., by and through its attorney Robinson & Associates, P.C., and for its Complaint against the Defendant states unto this Honorable Court as follows:

1. Plaintiff Robinson & Associates, P.C., is a corporate entity with its principal office in the city of Southfield, County of Oakland,

incorporated under the laws of the State of Michigan and conducts business in of the City of Southfield, Oakland County, Michigan.

2. Defendant Kim Rose Davis is a resident of Genesee County, Michigan.
3. The amount in controversy is $11,890.60, plus costs, statutory interest, and attorney fees, and is otherwise within the jurisdiction of this Court.
4. The transactions and/or occurrences giving rise to this Complaint arose in the City of Southfield, State of Michigan.

COMMON ALLEGATIONS

5. Plaintiff incorporates by reference the allegations contained in paragraphs 1–4 of this Complaint as though fully set forth therein.
6. Defendant entered into a Contingent Fee Agreement contract for legal services.

   Exhibit A.

   Robinson & Associates, P.C., thereafter filed a civil action on behalf of Kim Rose Davis in the United States District Court, Eastern District of Michigan, Case Number 08-12881-BC.
7. On March 26, 2009, a Settlement Conference was held with Federal Magistrate Judge Virginia Morgan. At that time, Kim Rose Davis agreed, on the record, to settle this case.

   Exhibit B.
8. Counsel for the Defendants in the USDC action forwarded the Settlement Agreement, Confidentiality Agreement, Indemnity Agreement For Derivative Claims And Release Of All Claims ("Release") on or about April 16, 2009.
9. Robinson & Associates, P.C., forwarded the Release to Kim R. Davis; however, she refused to speak directly to her attorneys and would not come in to the office or sign or return the Release.
10. On May 13, 2009, Robinson & Associates, P.C., filed a motion for order to enforce settlement and withdraw as counsel and at

a hearing before the Federal Judge on June 10, 2009, Defendant Davis admitted that she had agreed to release all claims in exchange for a settlement of $30,000.

11. Defendant Davis explained to the Court that her refusal to sign the written settlement agreement was because she did not have the opportunity to review the depositions of the Defendant police officers prior to the Settlement Conference. As a result of this hearing, Robinson & Associates, P.C., was directed to make the depositions available to her.

12. Robinson & Associates, P.C., forwarded the depositions to her on June 11, 2009, and at a continued hearing on July 6, 2009, Kim Rose Davis stated that she had received and reviewed the depositions prior to the hearing. On July 10, 2009, the Federal Court entered an Order Granting and Denying as Moot In Part Plaintiff's Motion to Enforce Settlement and Withdraw As Plaintiff's Counsel, Enforcing Settlement Agreement, Granting Defendants' Request For Costs, Directing Issue and Deposit of the Settlement Check, and Dismissing Plaintiff's Claim with Prejudice.

Exhibit C.

The Federal Court ordered the settlement check be deposited into a client trust account "pending resolution of the dispute with Ms. Davis."

14. Despite being given the opportunity to review the depositions, Kim Rose Davis still refuses to sign the Release and to endorse the settlement check received on August 5, 2000.

15. Defendant Davis continues to refuse to speak to her counsel and refuses to execute the Release and sign the settlement check to fulfill the terms of the Contingent Fee Agreement contract.

COUNT 1—BREACH OF CONTRACT

16. Plaintiff incorporates, by reference, the allegations contained in paragraphs 1–15 of this Complaint as though fully set forth therein.

17. Defendant Kim R. Davis's conduct amounts to a breach of the Contingent Fee Agreement contract signed by Defendant Davis on February 18, 2008.

Police, Lawyers & Judges

18. Plaintiff has suffered damages in an amount of $11,890.60, plus interest and the costs and attorney fees in bringing this action. WHEREFORE Plaintiff's counsel respectfully requests that this Court enter an Order granting the following relief:

A. Enforcing the settlement by ordering the costs and attorney fees arising from this action, plus $11,890.60, plus statutory interest from the date of this filing, be deducted from the settlement check and paid to Robinson & Associates, P.C.

1. Costs are $2,835.90

2. Attorney fee is $9,054.70

Exhibit D

Costs Sheet

B. Ordering the remaining balance payable to Defendant Davis be placed either in a Court escrow account or an interest-bearing client trust account.

Respectfully submitted,

David A. Robinson (P 38754)
Theophilus E. Clemons (P47991)
Attorneys for the Plaintiff
28145 Greenfield Road, Suite 100
Southfield, Michigan 48076
(248) 423-7234
August 24, 2009

This man is sick. He hid evidence from me. All I wanted from this case was cameras in the Buena Vista Police Department Vehicles. He lied to me, and the citizens of Buena Vista will still be terrorized by Timothy Wayne Patterson and Chief Brian Booker. I will see Mr. Robinson in court. Hasn't he figured out yet when GOD is for you, who could be against you?? The court date was set for December 8, 2009. Needless to say, David A. Robinson walked out of the 67th District Court the same way he entered: A LOSER!!! DAVID A. ROBINSON

HASN'T FIGURED OUT WHEN GOD IS FOR YOU, ALL THE CROOKED LAWYERS, CROOKED JUDGES, AND PROSECUTORS WILL FAIL IN TIME. MAYBE DAVID WILL CHANGE HIS WAYS. NOW I UNDERSTOOD WHY I WAS SILENT IN THE SETTLEMENT HEARING IN JUDGE MORGAN'S COURTROOM. GOD WANTED DAVID A. ROBINSON EXPOSED!!! I'm looking forward to my malpractice suit against David A. Robinson and Theophilus Clemons in 2010.

December 29, 2010. I finally received paperwork from my new attorney Riley P. Richards. He informed me that David A. Robinson was served, but Theophilus Clemons no longer worked in the same law firm with him. He was working elsewhere. He keeps running from his summons, but my attorney assured me that whatever it takes, Theophilus Clemons will be served. I was feeling good about my case.

January 10, 2011. I received paperwork from my attorney requesting documents from David A. Robinson's attorneys. I replied, and I was thinking to myself, *Let's get it on. I am ready to expose this man.*

March 9, 2011. I received a telephone call from my attorney. The first words out of his mouth were for me to settle my case and not take it to trial. I told him I wanted to go to trial. I wanted David A. Robinson and Theophilus Clemons to answer why they withheld evidence and lied to me under oath. He answered, "David A. Robinson has a good reputation."

I replied, "I don't care about his reputation. I want the truth." He sounded as if he didn't like my response, but I didn't care. It's about the truth, and I was entitled to it. He wouldn't expose to me the lying Police Officer Timothy Wayne Patterson who had a record. Now he must be exposed for what he is: a lying, conniving lawyer. We said our good-byes, and he informed me that he would be in touch real soon.

I called my attorney back on March 10, 2011, to tell him I was standing firm. I paid him $15,000, and I wanted David and Theophilus on the witness stand. I left this message on his voice mail. He wasn't in the office at the time.

On March 11, 2011, the *Jet* magazine arrived. On the front cover was Nia Long, turning 40. In the upper right-hand corner, it stated

Police, Lawyers & Judges

Phenomenal Sistas you need to know. I opened up the magazine to page 3 and saw five photos of powerful African-American women. The one that stuck out to me was Maya Angelou's. Her message to women was to develop your courage. I felt so empowered by reading her article. She wrote, "Once you have courage, you have a sense of your own value, and your other strengths will ensue!" I thanked her in my mind for writing that article. I needed to read this type of empowerment. My attorney wanted me to back down because of this man's reputation. "THANK YOU, GOD AND MAYA."

March 22, 2011. I received a letter from my attorney. It broke my heart. He was selling me down the drain. I had to sit down after reading this. My energy was gone. I didn't understand the legal system. This man was telling me if I didn't allow him to settle my case out of court, he was going to steal my $15,000 legally.

R: Davis v Clemons, et al

Dear Ms. Davis;

After a great deal of deliberation, I have decided to withdraw as your attorney in this matter. My decision to withdraw is largely based upon your insistence upon setting your claims for no less than $50,000 as to each of the attorneys. It is my firm belief that the likelihood of obtaining a settlement in that range is extremely unlikely to happen. It is my belief that any additional recovery beyond your prior settlement, although possible, is very problematic. It is more likely than not that you will not improve your position if the case proceeds to trial. The anticipated costs for expert witness fees, depositions, etc., could easily exceed $15,000 that you would be required to pay. In addition to retaining an attorney as your legal expert, you will also need an expert to testify as to the police misconduct.

In addition to the present litigation, I also provided representation for you in the attorney fee litigation brought by Robinson & Associates, P.C. This representation required two appearances in the district court, Flushing, Michigan. It also required the preparation of an answer to the Complaint, Jury Demand, and interrogatories.

Again, it is my strong recommendation that you settle your case at this time for whatever amounts the opposing parties are willing to pay.

To continue your case in the court system will undoubtedly end in a substantial loss.

Please contact me immediately upon receipt of this letter to discuss your options. If I do not receive a favorable response to my recommendation to allow me to negotiate a settlement, I will file a motion to withdraw as your attorney in this matter. I will also request the court to approve attorney fees for the representation provided to date at an hourly rate of $235.

Attorney Riley P. Richards

After reading this letter, my mother called. I read the letter to her. She asked me, "What are you going to do??"

"Nothing," I answered. "The race is over. I am going to work out."

"What do you mean work out?" she asked.

"I am going to the gym get on the treadmill and lift weights. I asked GOD to keep me from going to Livonia, Michigan, to kill that man." I thought, *How does this man feel he has the right to steal my money?* I didn't feel good about that, and I didn't understand the legal system. "Just as David lied and kept information, is this man is the same way?? Is there a course they're teaching in law school on how to cheat your clients?? And once you cheat them, you withdraw as their attorney?? I don't understand. I'll talk to you later, Mother. I must get to the gym."

March 26, 2011, 7 A.M. My phone was ringing off the hook. I answered the phone. It was my mother. She asked how was I feeling. "Fine," I answered. My mother then asked, "Do you have plans to fight him back?"

I answer, "No, I don't. I've been fighting since 2006. I'm tired. I am going to the gym."

My mother responded, "You should be getting a fight plan together instead of going to the gym."

I replied, "I don't have a plan; my only plan is to go running."

Mother responded, "You don't sound like my daughter."

I answered, "Mother, what can I do? He's going to steal my money."

She replied, "You can fight back."

I responded, "Okay, you give me a fight plan, and I will fight back!!!"

She replied, "Let me think about it, and don't forget you're bowling in the 700 Tournament tomorrow morning with my friend Walker. I'll see you at B's Bowling Center at 10:00 A.M."

Sunday, March 27. 2011. My mother arrived around 10:15 A.M. She was wearing a long red leather coat. She was saying something, but I couldn't understand what she was saying. As she got closer, I heard the words, "IT AIN'T OVER!!!" I was staring at her and didn't understand what she was talking about. She repeated it again.

I answered, "Of course, it's not over. I have two more games to bowl."

"NO NO NO!" she replied, and she took her seat. "Bishop T. D. Jakes said, 'IT AIN'T OVER!!!'

"As I was getting dressed for church this morning, I had the television on, listening to Bishop T. D. Jakes. He said when the enemy puts you in a corner with your back up against the wall, it ain't over. That is when GOD shows up and works that situation out for you."

Mama told me to FIGHT BACK!!!! I smiled. I knew when I finished bowling I would get my courage back. I prayed to GOD for his guidance to show me what steps to take.

Later that evening, he revealed to me what to do: write letters to the courts and one to the Federal Judge Ludington in Bay City, Michigan. He showed me favor before. Another letter was sent to a circuit court judge in Flint, Michigan. That judge and I used to attend the same church. I decided to have my sister Kathy type both letters for me. Once the letters were typed I delivered them personally. I drove to Bay City, Michigan, on March 29th. On the envelope to the federal judge, I wrote, "PLEASE HELP ME!!!!!!" in big bold letters. On my way home, I prayed that one of the judges would assist me.

On April 1, 2011, 12:30 P.M., I received a telephone call from my attorney Riley P. Richards telling me I can have depositions and he would represent me to the best of his ability. GOD is truly a wonderful GOD. Looking forward to seeing David and Theophilus in court.

I thanked GOD for meeting Martin Luther King Sr. When I shook his hand, I felt the power of my people singing "We Shall Overcome."

I know I did the Civil Rights movement proud for standing up for my rights, regardless that the predators were African-American. An injustice is wrong, no matter whom it comes from.

After my morning run, I checked the mail, and to my surprise, I received a letter from my attorney, Riley P. Richards. His jurisdiction # P23822.

I was excited and ready to face that villain in a court of law. To hire a lawyer and have him conceal evidence is one of the lowest things an attorney can do to his client. I was looking forward to hearing why this man chose to abandon me in my pursuit of justice. Only a man of no integrity would treat me in this manner.

July 29, 2011, as I prepared myself for my deposition, I prayed. I asked God to bless my memory, so that my words would be truthful, so I would represent myself to the best of my ability. As my mom and I drove to Livonia, Michigan, we were laughing and talking and having a good time. We arrived at Riley P. Richards's office 25 minutes early. We sat outside listening to music.

At 9:55, we walked into his office. We were greeted by a wonderful, friendly young lady that informed us that the opposing counsel would be about 20 minutes late. She and my mom engaged in friendly conversation. I took a seat facing the door. Twenty minutes passed, and I noticed a huge man climbing the stairwell. He lost his footing. He was able to stop his fall with his hand, but his papers were scattered all over the porch. Once he retrieved his paperwork, he came inside the office.

Mr. Richards informed me that he is the man whom we were waiting for. We went downstairs to the coldest room I've ever been in, in my life. My deposition was going along smoothly until he, opposing counsel, brought up that David A. Robinson of Southfield, Michigan, informed me that the police were given a deposition and that I forgot. I answered no, which seemed to anger him. He repeated it again, with a hint of intimidation in his voice. I put both my elbows on the table and looked this big bully in his eyes, and I answered "No!" We gave each other the stare down, as if two heavyweight champions were ready to square off in the ring. I don't know how long the stare down lasted, but he finally decided to ask me another question. I answered. The animosity between us seemed to leave for a second. Then he asked me if I was

RILEY P. RICHARD
ATTORNEY & COUNSELOR AT LAW
39040 W. Seven Mile Road
Livonia, MI 48152-1006

(734) 542-9500

July 7, 2011

Kim Davis

Re: Davis v Clemons, et al.

Dear Ms. Davis:

    Please find enclosed a copy of Plaintiff's Answer to Defendants' First Interrogatories and Second Interrogatories that were previously sent to you for your approval and signature. Please review all of the interrogatory answers to confirm that they are correct. If they are acceptable, please sign and return the signature page in the enclosed envelope.

    Your deposition remains scheduled for July 29, 2011 at 10:00 a.m. at my office. Again, please confirm your availability for the deposition and to discuss your anticipated deposition testimony.

    Mr. Robinson's deposition has been scheduled for August 16, 2011. You are permitted to attend. Additionally, I will ask Mr. Robinson any questions that you may have, if appropriate.

Respectfully,

Riley P. Richard

RPR/hd
Enclosures

writing a book. I answered yes. He asked for a copy of the book, and I told him sure.

With that, my attorney, Riley P. Richards, jumped in and said he didn't know that I was writing a book. I looked at him. I told this man during my second visit that I was writing a book about my experiences. Riley Richards had told me during that visit that my book should be taught in law schools so that attorneys would know how NOT to treat their clients. My deposition ended with BOTH Mr. Richards and Opposing Counsel asking me for a copy. I answered, "Sure, when the book comes out."

August 16, 2011

I drove to the office of Starr M. Kincaid # P57430, in Bloomfield Hills, Michigan. I was excited to see and hear what attorney David A. Robinson had to say about why he withheld info from me. Once again, I was 20 minutes early. I went inside and found the office on the second floor of Attorney Kincaid. I went inside and announced myself to the receptionist. She told me to have a seat and offered a magazine. Straight-up at 10:00 A.M. she called and announced me. The receptionist had a strange look on her face. She told me no one was there. I answered, "Yes, this is strange. My attorney Riley P. Richards isn't here." She made another phone call, and no one answered. She apologized to me, for my inconvenience. I told her it wasn't her fault. She decided to call Mr. Richards's office and ask why they didn't inform me of the cancelled meeting, but she ended up talking to the voice mail.

On my drive home, which is about an hour north of Bloomfield, my phone rang. I didn't answer and continued driving. I let it go to voice mail. Once I got home, I listened to my voice mail. It was Riley P. Richards's secretary, informing me that I needed to turn over my book before anything could be done. I started laughing. Who would turn over a book that is not complete? Yes, I was writing a book, but it wasn't completed, and also, the federal judge in Bay City, Michigan, gave me the clearance to write my book. He had more power than they do.

On Saturday, August 20, my sister and I were giving Mom a surprise 80th birthday party. I had a lot of running around to do pertaining to the party. So I decided to overlook Mr. Richards's demand for my book.

Later that day, my mom was so surprised, and everyone had a wonderful time.

Time passed and I never heard from Riley. Finally, I received paperwork from my attorney Mr. Richards.

After reading the letter, I started to laugh. Here is Riley P. Richards again, withdrawing as my attorney. This man has been trying to steal my money since March 2, 2011. I looked forward to seeing that crook, Riley P. Richards, in a court of law. I was praying that the judge I go before would be a judge that listened to all the evidence and had compassion in his heart for the truth.

October 14, 2011, arrived. I prayed and asked God for a safe journey back and forth from Detroit. As my mom and I traveled from Genesee County to Detroit, Michigan, we laughed, and we talked. I shared with her the song that I'd sung the previous night by the Rance Allen Group, "I'm Gonna Make It After All."

> I don't know
> what tomorrow gonna bring
> it may be sunshine
> and then again it may be rain
> All I know is I'm
> gonna make it after all.

My mom smiled and replied, "I give you credit, Kim, you love music, but God didn't bless you with a voice. But I love you in spite of that."

We were walking toward the Coleman A. Young Municipal Center, 2 Woodward Avenue, Detroit, Michigan. As we made our way toward the elevator, I was feeling excited. I was looking forward to standing before a female judge. All the other judges were males. This was going to be interesting. I looked forward to presenting my case in COURTROOM 1107.

I arrived 10 minutes early to the courtroom of the Honorable Kathleen MacDonald, bar # 38029. Finally, the bailiff unlocked the door. In

RILEY P. RICHARD
ATTORNEY AND COUNSELOR AT LAW
39040 WEST SEVEN MILE ROAD
LIVONIA, MICHIGAN 48152-1006

(734) 542-9500
FAX (734) 542-0057
Malpracticelaw@ameritech.net

September 22, 2011

Ms. Kim Davis

Re: Davis v Robinson, et al.

Dear Ms. Davis:

As a consequence of your failure to provide a copy of the "book" authored by you regarding the underlying events of this litigation, Defendants have filed a Motion for Involuntary Dismissal as well as other relief. A copy of the Motion and exhibits is attached.

I am again requesting that you provide me with a copy of your "book" to be provided to opposing counsel. A protective order is in place prohibiting Defendants from disclosing or otherwise distributing the contents of your book.

If you do not produce a copy of the book, it is virtually certain that the court will dismiss your lawsuit. Further, because the discovery order was not complied with, the court at minimum will likely award attorney fees to Defendants.

Again, I am requesting that you contact me to discuss this matter in detail.

Also enclosed is a Motion to Withdraw as your attorney in this matter. This Motion is scheduled for October 7, 2011.

Respectfully,

Riley P. Richard

Enclosures

RPR/jl

the words of the Temptations, "I'm on cloud nine." I had my paperwork in my hand, I had prayed, and I was ready to fight the good fight.

As my mother and I took our seats, I noticed a Caucasian female looking back at me several times. I started to wonder, who is this woman, and why does she have me on her radar. Finally, she stopped looking back at me, then in walked the liar from Livonia, Michigan: Riley P. Richards. He immediately sat down next to this woman that kept glancing toward me. I noticed they engaged in some type of conversation.

After maybe two or three cases were presented, I heard *Riley P. Richards vs. Kim Davis*. As I walked toward the defendant spot, I noticed this short, small-statured Caucasian woman grab the defendant podium, looking back at me as if she's the cat that swallowed the canary. I stopped walking and started to turn around and go back to my seat. I was under the impression that a mistake was made, that when I thought I heard my name, they called this woman's name instead. The young lady that I thought I heard called my name and beckoned me to come forward, nodding her head yes.

Once I approached the bench, I stood next to this short, Caucasian woman. To my surprise, Judge Kathleen MacDonald told me to move. I stared at her for a couple of seconds, not able to comprehend who this woman was and why I had to move and not her. I stood there for a short period, and the judge still motioned for me to move. She had me stand next to Mr. Richards, the man who was trying to steal my money. I was stunned and confused. This should be illegal!

As I was walking back to my seat, I looked at my mother and told her, "This was as if I was in the Twilight Zone." I've never seen a tag team effect in a courtroom, only on TV, watching wrestling. As I exited the courtroom, Riley P. Richards was standing next to this woman that intruded in my case. I learned that her name is Starr Kincaid. I ask Mr. Richards for some of my money back, that the case was not completed. This short man answered with, "When I finish with you, you won't have nothing left!" He glanced over at Kincaid, and they smiled. At that time, I realized how good God is. I was able to walk away from those two snakes in the grass with the grace and dignity that I was taught from my mother, my two deceased grandmothers, Lenora Black and Nelly Packer, and my great-aunts, the Woodson women.

```
1                    STATE OF MICHIGAN
2           IN THE CIRCUIT COURT FOR THE COUNTY OF WAYNE
3
    KIM ████ DAVIS,
4
              Plaintiff,        Case No. 10-011-806-NM
5   vs.
6   DAVID ROBINSON,
7             Defendant.
    ---------------------------/
8
9             Proceedings taken in the above-entitled
10  matter before **HONORABLE KATHLEEN MACDONALD,** Third
11  Judicial Circuit Court Judge, Detroit, Michigan, on
12  Friday, October 14, 2011.
13
    APPEARANCES:
14
15  ON BEHALF OF THE PLAINTIFF:    MR. RILEY P. RICHARD
16
17
    ON BEHALF OF THE DEFENDANT:    MS. STARR M. KINCAID
18
19
20
21  Also present:  Ms. Kim Rose Davis
22
23
24
    Shelee Beard
25  Official Court Reporter
```

```
 1                    Detroit, Michigan
 2                    Friday, October 14, 2011
 3                         - - -
 4              THE CLERK:  Calling case number
 5     10-011806, Davis versus Robinson.
 6              MS. KINCAID:  Good morning, your
 7     Honor, Starr Kincaid on behalf of the defendant.
 8              MR. RICHARD:  Good morning, your
 9     Honor.  Riley Richard on behalf of the plaintiff.
10     This is my motion to withdraw as counsel for Kim
11     Davis.  This origin of this case was a legal
12     malpractice case.  We had Ms. Davis' deposition
13     during the course of this litigation.  It was
14     discovered she was in the process of having a
15     book she had written about her experiences.  I
16     was not aware of this.
17              They demanded a copy of the book.  I
18     believe the book would be discoverable with
19     restriction on the book.  I indicated that to Ms.
20     Davis.  We didn't have communication.  I agreed
21     to an order for the production of the book with
22     restriction that it could not be disclosed beyond
23     any purpose of this Court.  I sent it to Ms.
24     Davis, sent her letters, and I got no response.
25              I filed this motion to withdraw.  I
```

feel there's been a breakdown on this with respect to my ability to represent Ms. Davis.

THE COURT: Okay. Ms. Davis, do you have anything to say.

PLAINTIFF DAVIS: Yes, I do. The federal judge in Bay City, Judge Ludington, knew that I was writing a book. He said I did not have to sign a confidentiality clause, to write my book and to make sure I wrote the truth.

THE COURT: Yeah.

PLAINTIFF DAVIS: And that's what I'm doing. Is the book finished? No, it is not.

THE COURT: Whatever you have done you need to produce.

PLAINTIFF DAVIS: Even though Judge Ludington said I didn't have to sign a confidentiality clause?

THE COURT: I think you're talking about a whole different case.

PLAINTIFF DAVIS: No, I'm not.

THE COURT: I'm granting your motion to withdraw. There will be a 30-day stay on the case for you to get another attorney. A status conference will take place 7 days after expiration of the 30 days. And, Ms. Davis, put

```
                                                              5

 1        your phone number, address, and how we can reach
 2        you into the order, so we'll have it.
 3                PLAINTIFF DAVIS:  I paid this man
 4        $15,000 to represent me in this case.  He has not
 5        completed the case.  Am I awarded my money back?
 6                THE COURT:  That's between you and
 7        him.
 8                PLAINTIFF DAVIS:  Okay.
 9                MS. KINCAID:  Your Honor, with
10        respect to --
11                THE COURT:  I know you have your
12        motion pending, but I have to adjourn it.
13                MS. KINCAID:  I anticipated that.
14        With respect to the withdrawal, I don't have any
15        objections.  We would just like to reserve the
16        right to pursue frivolous action against
17        plaintiff and her counsel.
18                THE COURT:  Status conference will be
19        November 30th.
20                MS. KINCAID:  Will that be at 9?
21                THE COURT:  Yes.
22                MR. RICHARD:  Can I submit the order
23        under the 7-day rule, your Honor?
24                THE COURT:  Yes.
25                (Whereupon proceedings concluded.)
```

On the drive home, my mom said to me, "I have never been in such a courtroom that was run with pure racism and hatred." She asked me if I felt I could win my case in Judge Kathleen MacDonald's courtroom.

I answered "No, but I'm going down swinging."

November 10, 2011, I appeared back in Judge Kathleen's courtroom. As I took my seat, I was going over my paperwork. A man sat to the left of me. He wore a nice blue suit and had on nice shoes and socks. He smelled so good I had to check him out thoroughly. We engaged in light conversation. He asked me if I was a lawyer. I answered "No," then I shared with him my story. When I finished, he apologized to me. He told me he was sorry for what happened to me. He also told me he didn't let people know he was a lawyer because 90 percent of lawyers are crooks. He told me he was embarrassed to share with people what he did for a living. This gentleman told me to keep my head up and to fight the best fight of my life. We shook hands, and then I heard Attorney Riley P. Richards's and my name being called. I glanced around. As I walked to the defendant's position, I looked for Starr Kincaid and was happy she was not there.

As Riley began to speak, he said nothing bad about me. He said I had a mind of my own, and once it's made up, it's hard to change it, and that's why he was withdrawing as my attorney. Judge Kathleen MacDonald was looking toward Riley, and she seemed to be listening to him. Finally, it was my time to speak. I held up the letter, and I said, "This man has been trying to steal my money since March 20th of this year. This man has not completed the case, and I have the proof right here." I noticed that Judge Kathleen MacDonald had her head down. I was shocked. I had another letter to show her where the judge in Flushing, Michigan, ruled for Mr. Richards not to charge me. I had paperwork proving that. Judge Kathleen kept her head down. She did not look at my evidence. She refused to look at me. Finally, she lifted her head up and said, "Case dismissed. You all can leave." I was stunned by this judge's unprofessional attitude.

On November 30, 2011, I met Starr Kincaid. I didn't understand what that was about. It was a beautiful morning. I decided to stand and look out of the window of Judge Kathleen MacDonald's courtroom #1107. My mother was seated with her back against the window. In walked Starr M. Kincaid. She walked up to my mother and me as if

Police, Lawyers & Judges

she and I were best friends. She said Riley P. Richards filed paperwork that gave them the right to my unpublished book. I turned and glanced back out the window. I knew proper protocol. Mr. Richards cannot overrule a federal judge. So I was done and had nothing else to say to this woman. She mentioned this again. My mother answered her, "Riley can't overrule a federal judge, I know proper protocol."

Starr answered my mother that Riley could overrule a federal judge. I was laughing on the inside. Ms. Kincaid was living up to what I think of lawyers. *Liars!* Finally, my mother and Starr stopped their verbal tug-of-war. Kincaid and I were called back to the chambers of Judge MacDonald. Ms. Kincaid was seated to my right. Judge MacDonald was in front of us at her desk. Out of the blue, this woman looked at me with pure hatred and told me, "Don't say anything. It can and will be used against you!"

I looked at this judge and thought to myself, *How blessed she is that I was raised to be a Christian woman. If not, I would jam my fist down her throat and pull her tonsils out.* But I had to sing to myself, "Oh, how I love Jesus," over and over and over again, to calm myself down. Now I understand why I'm in this woman's courtroom—not for justice. She has aligned herself with whatever they want to do me. She's onboard. I'm not only fighting corrupt lawyers, it's as if this woman is Satan's sister.

As I left her chambers, I turned to give her one last look. She was looking at me as if she and I were in a battle—not me and the lawyers.

On December 2, 2011, Attorney Riley P. Richards and I were back in Judge Kathleen MacDonald's courtroom. She gave Riley everything he wanted. He could withdraw as my attorney, and he could keep my $15,000. She had a smirk on her face. I raised my hand, asking, "How can you award this man $15,000 to quit a case? When I tried to show you proof, you wouldn't look at it."

She hollered back toward me, "You didn't get your evidence in on time."

I stood there stunned, looking at this lady. *Unbelievable,* I thought to myself. I remembered an important fact. He did not put all the lawyers' names on his paperwork. He had blacked out some of them. As I was ready to say that, Riley P. Richards said, "Your Honor, the reason I left counsels' names blacked out, I thought you might not have wanted to read their names." She answered it didn't matter. It looked good to her.

Date	Description	Hours
10/23/09	Corr /fax to Atty. Robinson	0.3
10/29/09	T/C - Atty. Robinson	0.2
10/30/09	T/C - Atty. Robinson; Corr to Atty. Robinson	0.4
11/03/09	T/C - Dawn Stone re Davis file; email from Dawn Stone; review of Order Granting Motion to Enforce Settlement	0.4
11/06/09	Court Appearance – Pre-trial; Preparation of 1st request of Production of Documents; preparation of Interrogatories to Robinson; preparation of Notice of Deposition; Proof of Service David	3.5
12/04/09	O/C - Client	1.0
12/08/09	Corr to Client	0.2
12/14/09	Corr to Atty. Robinson – Stip. of Dismissal	0.2
12/18/09	Corr to Atty. Robinson	0.2
01/05/10	Receipt of Robinson & Assoc. Order of Dismissal	0.2
03/08/10	T/C - Atty. ▇	0.2
03/10/10	T/C - Atty. ▇; T/C - Client; T/C - Atty. ▇	0.4
03/16/10	T/C - Atty. ▇	0.2
04/14/10	T/C - Atty. ▇	0.3
04/19/10	T/C - Atty. ▇; T/C - Atty. ▇	0.3
04/20/10	T/C – Atty. ▇; T/C - Atty. ▇; T/C - Atty. ▇ email from Atty. ▇	0.6
05/06/10	Review file – research regarding expert witness	0.5
05/12/10	T/C - John G. Peters	0.2
06/09/10	T/C - ▇ L/M	0.1
06/11/10	T/C - Atty ▇	0.2

She looked at him and said, "Everything is correct; you're entitled to that money." I felt robbed. He can quit my case *and* keep my money. What kind of justice is this? Did she become a judge to do favors for friends and destroy people's lives? She must be a bitter, lonely lady.

December 16, 2011. This is the day that I get to face Starr Kincaid. A friend of mine met me at court. He had been in front of Judge MacDonald before. He and some of his friends were all on the same page as I. She was an evil, bitter female.

The first case was called. It was between an attractive, well dressed, tall African-American attorney against two Caucasian female attorneys. One female stood in the plaintiff position; he stood in the defendant's position. There was another female standing to the right of the black male. I watched and wondered, is this how she runs her court, allowing African-Americans to be tag teamed. The female plaintiff spoke first, and then the man spoke. Before the other woman with the female plaintiff could finish her sentence, the African-American male spoke in a voice of outrage. He pointed to the female to the right of him and asked the judge, "Who is this woman, and why is she speaking?" The judge was silent. The male attorney asked the question again, as loud as he could, "Who is she?"

Judge Kathleen MacDonald answered in a bizarre manner and said there was a case that had come before her and she thought she had the right to overrule a federal judge. The federal judge that she overruled personally called her and informed her she couldn't overrule his ruling. She started to lightly laugh. The courtroom was quiet and stunned. I thought to myself, *There's my opening. I will make sure I use the federal judge when I present my case before Judge MacDonald.*

Finally, our names were called, Starr Kincaid on behalf of the defendant, Kim Davis for the plaintiff. As I walked toward the podium, I waited for Kincaid to reach her podium. To my surprise, she walked up to the podium, running her mouth.

December 16, 2011. Davis/Kincaid

Judge Kathleen MacDonald dismissed my case. I readied myself to leave. Starr Kincaid asked, "Are you going to wait for your paperwork?"

```
 1                    STATE OF MICHIGAN

 2         IN THE CIRCUIT COURT FOR THE COUNTY OF WAYNE

 3
       KIM      DAVIS,
 4
                  Plaintiff,        Case No. 10-011806-NM
 5     vs.

 6     DAVID ROBINSON, et. al,

 7                  Defendants.
       ---------------------------/
 8

 9              Proceedings taken in the above-entitled

10     matter before **HONORABLE KATHLEEN MACDONALD**, Third

11     Judicial Circuit Court Judge, Detroit, Michigan, on

12     Friday, December 16, 2011.

13
       APPEARANCES:
14

15     ON BEHALF OF PLAINTIFF:   MS. KIM     DAVIS, Pro per

16

17

18
       ON BEHALF OF DEFENDANT:   MS. STARR KINCAID (P57430)
19

20

21

22

23

24
       Shelee Beard
25     Official Court Reporter
```

```
                                                              3

 1                       Detroit, Michigan
 2                    Friday, December 16, 2011
 3                            - - -
 4             THE CLERK:  Calling case number
 5   10-011806, Davis versus Robinson.
 6             MS. KINCAID:  Starr Kincaid on behalf
 7   of the defendant.
 8             MS. DAVIS:  Kim Davis for the
 9   plaintiff.
10             MS. KINCAID:  This is defendant's
11   motion for involuntary dismissal.  The impetus
12   for this motion is the repeated discovery
13   violations by plaintiff throughout this matter as
14   well as woeful violation of a Court order.  The
15   Court order relates to a book that plaintiff
16   authored regarding what she testified to was the
17   truth of her underlying claim in this legal
18   malpractice action.  We didn't discover until her
19   deposition that the book existed despite
20   discovery requests prior to that as well as a
21   Notice of Deposition Duces Tecum indicating that
22   all such materials should be produced.
23             At the deposition we discovered the
24   book existed.  After several attempts to obtain
25   the book as for more specifically identified in
```

```
 1    my notes and the supporting brief, an order was
 2    entered August 18th to compel the book by August
 3    29th.  As of this date, we still don't have the
 4    book.  And there is still refusal to produce the
 5    book.  In this case, there's been repeated
 6    failure to cooperate in the discovery process.
 7    It's delayed the case.  More than likely we have
 8    to continue plaintiff's deposition.  Defendant's
 9    deposition was scheduled but had to be adjourned.
10    Expert depositions were scheduled, had to be
11    adjourned.  Plaintiff's former counsel withdraw,
12    so things were moved back to give her to get the
13    counsel.  I understand that hasn't happened as of
14    this date.  That's her prerogative.
15            We've had to file several discovery
16    motions throughout this case or tried to obtain
17    stipulation and order to get discovery this case.
18    Then to find out later that discovery exists that
19    we weren't provided.  And then not to be able to
20    get that discovery, despite a Court order, it's
21    simply unwarranted, willful violation and willful
22    noncompliance that has prejudiced defendant, your
23    Honor.
24            The pattern of discovery abuse should
25    not be tolerated.  It certainly warrants a
```

1   voluntary dismissal in this case. We have cost
2   and attorney fees for having to file this motion.
3   This is the second time we've had to file because
4   it was filed immediately prior to plaintiff's
5   former counsel to withdraw. As a courtesy we
6   allowed all the motions to be heard at once in
7   the even she were to retain new counsel.
8   MS. DAVIS: May I speak now?
9   THE COURT: Yes.
10   MS. DAVIS: Yes. The reason they
11 were never given a copy of the book is because
12 the federal judge in Bay City did not force me to
13 sign a confidentiality clause. The reason being
14 is because David A. Robinson, the man she
15 represents, withheld depositions from me, from
16 the police. He withheld four different
17 depositions. The one deposition one of the
18 police officers had a record, which Mr. Robinson
19 chose to hide from me. So, therefore, the higher
20 Court said you not have to sign any paperwork.
21 He also told me to write my book, make sure i
22 write the truth. That's all I have done.
23 Everything I have written I have --
24   THE COURT: That has nothing to do
25 with whether you're going to produce this or not.

Are you going to produce the book?

        MS. DAVIS: No.

        THE COURT: Case is dismissed. Your motion is granted.

        MS. KINCAID: Thank you, your Honor. I did prepare an order.

        (Whereupon proceedings concluded.)

- - -

```
'E OF MICHIGAN )
              ) SS
ITY OF WAYNE  )


     R E P O R T E R' S   C E R T I F I C A T E


         I, Shelee Beard, CSR-5493, do hereby
ify that I have recorded the proceedings had and
imony taken in the above-entitled matter at the
 and place hereinbefore set forth and that the
going is a full, true and correct transcript of
eedings had in the above-entitled matter; and I do
her certify that the foregoing transcript has been
ared by me or under my direction.
```

              Shelee D. Beard
           Shelee D. Beard, CSR-5493
           1107 Coleman A. Young Municipal Center
           Detroit, MI 48226
           (313) 224-5225

I realized I made a fatal mistake when I answered, "No, I'm not. I'm going downstairs to file paperwork to have my case heard in a higher court."

She looked at me, surprised. As we left the courtroom, I took one last look at Judge Kathleen MacDonald. I hope to never see or hear her voice ever again in this lifetime. She's rotten, and no one deserves to be in courtroom 1107 as long as she's presiding. As I filed my paperwork to have my case heard in a higher court, I received paperwork that Judge MacDonald dismissed my case with prejudice.

Proverbs 18:5: "It's wrong to favor the guilty and keep the innocent from getting justice" (Contemporary English Version).

When I received this paperwork about 2 weeks later, I was stunned and at a loss for words. I asked God to lead and guide me. I was not done with Judge Kathleen MacDonald, but I didn't know what to do.

The last week of March 2012, I decided to run outdoors. I'm free when I'm outside. My mind seems to have a better balance of things.

March 25, 2012. Tiger Woods wins. That inspired me for what I had to do.

On Tuesday, March 27, as I was running at Hamady High School, I heard the word *March*. I looked around, but I didn't see anyone else there. So I didn't understand where this voice was coming from. I ran that whole week and heard the word *march* the whole week.

As I was running on April 2, 2012, I was still hearing the word *march*, but I didn't understand what I was supposed to do. The only marching I've done before was in front of General Motors when we were on strike. I was retired from GM, so I didn't understand why I kept hearing the word *march*.

I went again Tuesday morning to do more running, and I saw a baby deer near the fence. I stopped running, walked toward the fence, and talked to the deer. As I was about to reach toward the deer to pet it, I heard a crackling sound. To my surprise, it was the mother deer. She had the look only a mother could have when protecting her child, so I started back running. The two of them disappeared. To my surprise, I saw a deer in full stride, running toward the track where I was at. I had left my dog spray in the car. So I ran toward the other end of the track to try to climb the fence to get away from this angry deer. She charged toward the track, and I was frightened.

STATE OF MICHIGAN

IN THE CIRCUIT COURT FOR THE COUNTY OF WAYNE

KIM ROSE DAVIS
    Plaintiff,

v

Case No. 10-011806-NM
Hon. Kathleen Macdonald

DAVID A. ROBINSON, and
ROBINSON & ASSOCIATES, P.C.
    Defendants.

_____/

RILEY P. RICHARD (P23822)
Attorney for Plaintiff
39040 West Seven Mile Road
Livonia, MI 48152-1006
(734) 542-9500

Lipson, Neilson, Cole, Seltzer & Garin, P.C.
By: Phillip E. Seltzer (P34530)
Starr M. Kincaid (P57430)
Attorneys for Defendants David A. Robinson and
David A. Robinson & Associates, P.C.
3910 Telegraph Rd., Ste. 200
Bloomfield Hills, MI 48302
(248) 593-5000

_____/

MOTION FOR APPROVAL OF ATTORNEY FEES

NOW COMES Riley P. Richard, former attorney for Plaintiff, Kim Rose Davis and states as follows:

1. On September 1, 2009, Plaintiff, Kim Rose Davis ("Davis"), retained Riley P. Richard ("Richard") to provide legal representation regarding claims against Theopolous E. Clemons, David A. Robinson, and Robinson & Associates, P.C.
2. The parties executed a Fee Agreement whereby Richard would be paid the greater of one-third (1/3) of the net recovery or $15,000.00.
3. Richard has spent in excess of 75 hours in providing legal representation to Davis.
4. Richard's withdrawal as the attorney for Davis was for good cause.
5. The Contingency Fee Agreement further provided for Richard to be compensated at a rate of $250.00 per hour.
6. Richard has incurred costs in the amount of $678.90 as a result of representing Davis.

To my amazement, she got right to the fence and stopped. I had my hands on the fence, ready to climb if she jumped over. Instead, she turned and ran away. With that, I started thanking the Lord as I clapped my hands, elated. All of a sudden, I heard the word *march* again.

I got in my car and drove to a place of business that I had never been before. I asked the owner, "Do you make signs?"

He asked me what type of sign I was looking for. I answered, "Signs pertaining to a corrupt judge."

He answered, "Yes, I will make your signs, and I will make them sturdy so that you can hold them when the wind blows."

As I turned to leave, I asked him, "Are you sure you know what I need?"

He said, "Yes," with a big grin on his face. "You're doing an old-school march, and I'm happy to help any way I can."

Wednesday on the 4th of April, I was invited to a bowling banquet by L. C. Before I left to attend the banquet, my mother called. She wanted me to come to church that evening at Antioch Baptist Church on Stewart Street, where the pastor is Louis Randolph. She wanted me to hear this man badly, and to my surprise, once I arrived at the banquet, L. C. told me he's singing in the choir tonight at Antioch Baptist Church. So I thought to myself, *I'm going to go.*

That evening as I took my seat, I saw other bowling friends there to support L. C. Rev. Dr. Tellis J. Chapman of Galilee Missionary Baptist Church was speaking at the revival. I enjoyed his sermon as he's a wonderful speaker, then he stunned me. Toward the end of his sermon, he said, "Sometimes, we have to go and march for our rights. Nothing is wrong with marching." I had to contain myself. I was ready to do cartwheels in the aisles of the church. I knew that I was on the right track to hear this man of God speak on marching.

April 10, 2012. I was talking with my bowling partner by the name of Carnell Smith. I shared with him that I was not going to do any summer bowling. Instead, I was going to march. He looked at me and gave me the biggest smile. He said, "Kim, I marched in the '60s with the late Dr. Martin Luther King Jr. Dr. King came down South and spoke to us. Kim, I will march with you."

And I looked at him and said, "Guess what?"

He answered "What?" and I shared with him that I had met Martin Luther King Sr. in 1977. We stood up and gave each other a high five and said, "May God be with us."

The first day I marched with my mom and Carnell Smith was April 18th. My mom was excited, even though she can't march (she had a bad back and had to sit in a chair). But she was eagerly waiting to hold a sign that read, "Do Not Reelect Kathleen MacDonald!"

As we drove to Detroit, everyone was upbeat and excited about doing our part for civil rights. As Carnell and I were marching around the courthouse, we were stopped by a young man that wanted to take pictures of our signs. I asked him why. He told us that Judge Kathleen MacDonald heard that someone was outside carrying signs with her name on them. She wanted to read what they said. He took pictures of our signs. Before he left, I asked him to make sure he told Judge Kathleen MacDonald that I was marching against her because she was an unjust judge to me.

He asked, "What's your name?"

I answered, "Kim Davis. Better yet, take my picture."

He did.

After we finished marching we were excited at all the people that blew horns or stopped to talk to us about the injustice that they had received in different courts. Some people as they were exiting the courthouse asked if I could march for them. I shared with them I couldn't march for them, I could only march for my own injustice, and that I would be lying if I carried a sign with other judges' names and not had witnessed their injustice.

On April 23, 2012, I received my letter from the judicial tenure commission. Of course, they refused to do anything about the judge.

I ran to find my letter that I received when I had written the attorney grievance commission. It's mind-boggling to me how corrupt lawyers and judges are. There needs to be a commission made up of other people instead of their friends that are just as corrupt as they are.

May 3, 2012, I received a letter from Riley P. Richards stating that I better go downtown Detroit and apologize to him for the sign that reads "Judge Kathleen MacDonald allowed Riley Richards, P23822, to steal $15,000 from me." Well, I had the right to carry the sign because of the First Amendment. Judge Kathleen MacDonald violated my constitutional

COMMISSIONERS		PAUL J. FISCHER, ESQ.
		EXECUTIVE DIRECTOR
THOMAS J. RYAN, ESQ.		& GENERAL COUNSEL
CHAIRPERSON		
HON. NANCI J. GRANT		3034 W. GRAND BLVD., STE. 8-450
VICE CHAIRPERSON		CADILLAC PLACE BUILDING
HON. DAVID H. SAWYER		DETROIT, MICHIGAN 48202
SECRETARY		TELEPHONE (313) 875-5110
HON. PABLO CORTES		FAX (313) 875-5154
NANCY J. DIEHL, ESQ.		
DAVID T. FISCHER	State of Michigan	
HON. JOHN D. HAMILTON	Judicial Tenure Commission	
BRENDA L. LAWRENCE		
HON. JEANNE STEMPIEN		

April 17, 2012

Kim Rose Davis

RE: Request for Investigation No. 2012-19762

Dear Ms. Davis:

    The Judicial Tenure Commission has completed the investigation conducted at your request. The Commission's jurisdiction is limited to determining whether there is evidence of judicial misconduct, as that term is defined by law. The Commission has determined that there is no basis for commencing formal disciplinary proceedings or taking any other action. Accordingly, the file in this matter has been closed. Thank you for bringing this matter to the Commission's attention.

                                    Sincerely,

                                    Paul J. Fischer
                                    Executive Director and
                                    General Counsel

PJF/cat

Police, Lawyers & Judges 195

rights by avoiding my Eighth and Fourteenth Amendment. I laughed to myself. This man was out of his mind. He had stolen my $15,000, and now he thought he had the right to tell me what I can and can't do. I was determined to march for as long as I chose to, and I would carry the sign with his name on it. If he didn't like it, he could come and stop me.

For reasons I didn't understand, I decided to make a video and put it on YouTube. I shared this with my sister. She told me of a friend of hers who is a minister and videographer that goes to her church. His name was Theodore Files, and he said he would help me. We picked a date and time that he was willing to ride with us to Detroit and film us in front of the courthouse. I decided that I needed to film where I had the pleasure of meeting Dr. Martin Luther King Sr., so I asked the minister of Kent St. Church of God, which used to be named Grace Emmanuel Baptist Church, for permission to do so. The minister was stunned when I spoke to him and asked if I could use his church to film inside. No one had ever shared with him that Dr. King Sr. had been in his pulpit! All he wanted from me was a copy of the bulletin.

I was thankful for his kindness. Then I decided to call a friend of mind, Elder Dana Chaney. We used to work together in Saginaw, Michigan. I made the phone call. He was willing, ready, and able. We met at Kent St. Church of God and filmed our video. Everyone was excited and happy. I was surprised at myself. Normally, I was shy, quiet, and reserved. But this journey that I have embarked on seemed to be changing me. Now, I was more outgoing. In a million years you never could have told me I would be making a video. But with God, all things are possible.

One day as Carnell and I were marching in Detroit, we noticed news trucks there. They were Channel 2, Channel 4, Channel 7, and the Internet news. As I walked up to each truck, I asked how I could get a story on TV about Judge Kathleen MacDonald. I was given cards by all of them telling me to e-mail them my story. I e-mailed all of them, but never received a reply from any of them. Even my own local, 659, wouldn't do a story. But with God, all things are possible.

The young man that videoed me marching in Detroit, Theodore Files, informed me that he was a writer for his church's newspaper, which is called the *Temple Epistle*, published by Greater Holy Temple

COGIC in Flint, Michigan, at 6702 Dort Highway, where Bishop Roger Jones is the pastor.

My marching finally came to a halt due to the sickness of my father. God has told us to honor our mother and father. I would continue to march and speak out against corruption that runs through our judicial system. My fight was just beginning. I would continually speak out against injustice in the court system. I would wonder for as long as I live how many people are unjustly in jail and prison. This is my journey for justice. Remember to always acknowledge God and God will direct thy paths.

The Epilogue

I HAVE PATIENTLY BEEN WAITING FOR MY BOOK TO BE RELEASED FOR 2 YEARS. My pastor recommended a church member to publish my book. He shared with my mother he would have the book edited, and that's all he would do. He was e-mailed the book during August–September 2012. For reasons I don't understand, it is already 2013, and still, nothing has come from him. Recently, I received a phone call from him, telling me God had placed something on his heart concerning me. I shared with my mother thinking, "I'm finally going to get my book edited and go to print." The day of the meeting was for the 7th of February at 7:30 A.M.

As I showered that morning, I prayed and asked God to watch over me and allow me to represent his glory, to mind my tongue and my spirit, and to represent him to the best of my ability. During the meeting at Coney Island, I showed the pastor my receipt for paying the lady he recommended $5,000. He put on his glasses and looked at the receipt. He handed me back the receipt, put his glasses away, and positioned himself in an aggressive manner. Both elbows on the table, he leaned forward and said, "I'm going to apologize to you because you feel I owe you one." He continued, "I came to the bowling alley because I had a meeting with you. For reasons I can't explain, her name came up, and you didn't do your due diligence. You were supposed to read something by her, look at her work. You would have found out that her grammar was horrible. I couldn't read her work, her grammar was terrible. As far as me getting your book edited, I looked online. They have book editors in other states. I didn't see any in Michigan, so I won't be getting your book edited." And he stared me straight in my eyes.

I was stunned, so I took an aggressive stance against him. My reply was, "Number 1, I did not have a meeting with you at B's Bowling Center. You came to me, asking me what I was going to do with my book. I told you, my sister and I were online looking for a publisher. You shared with me you had a publisher at the church. You told me her name and what she looked like. I took that as your endorsement of her. You didn't share that you had never read anything by her.

"And another thing, I equated you with the late Lindell L. Brady. He never would have come to me without checking out the situation first. He would have read something by her and when the late Rev. Lindell L. Brady endorsed someone, it was money in the bank."

He fell back against the seat. I told him I would get my book done sometime this year. I didn't need his help. I gathered my belongings to leave. He stopped me and asked me if I would be willing to bowl with the church team for Big Brothers and Big Sisters. I was stunned!

I answered, "No." He has two good bowlers in his church. He didn't need me. I left. As I sat in my car, I didn't understand why he called me and said God had placed this on his heart. God is a God of solutions not confusion.

As I left the meeting, I was determined to have my book published by any means necessary. To all you readers who have read my journey through all this turmoil, remember, as long as you have God on your side and don't lose faith, you will receive your blessings in due time. People in the positions of power sometimes will step on your constitutional rights because they think they can get away with injustice, so please be mindful of your rights that were given to you by the Constitution.

On June 22, 2013, in Detroit, Michigan, it was a privilege and an honor to go with the UAW and participate in the Fiftieth Anniversary of the March to Freedom. I was able to walk the same route as the late Dr. Martin Luther King, Jr., the late Rev. C. L. Franklin, the late Walter Reuther, and it will always hold a special place in my heart. Without them marching for freedom and justice, I never would have fought the corruption as I did.

Peace and Love
Sister Kim Davis